SpringerBriefs in Finance

More information about this series at http://www.springer.com/series/10282

Navin Kumar

Chronic Regulatory Focus and Financial Decision-Making

Asset and Portfolio Allocation

Springer

Navin Kumar
Queensland University of Technology
Brisbane, QLD
Australia

ISSN 2193-1720 ISSN 2193-1739 (electronic)
SpringerBriefs in Finance
ISBN 978-981-287-693-5 ISBN 978-981-287-694-2 (eBook)
DOI 10.1007/978-981-287-694-2

Library of Congress Control Number: 2015946593

Springer Singapore Heidelberg New York Dordrecht London

Printed on acid-free paper

Springer Science+Business Media Singapore Pte Ltd. is part of Springer Science+Business Media (www.springer.com)

Preface

Behavioural finance explores the various anomalies that exist within financial markets, but does not provide insights into the motivations that drive these phenomena. Merely documenting such phenomena is insufficient, and studying the motivations behind these decisions will provide greater understanding into how and why such occurrences take place. A psychological theory, regulatory focus theory, has been applied to gain insight into the motivations that underlie one's financial decisions. Regulatory focus theory explores the relationship between the motivation of a person and their means of goal pursuit. Regulatory focus refers to how one approaches pleasure, but avoids pain. There are two regulatory foci, promotion and prevention. The promotion focus is on hopes and accomplishments (gains), and the prevention focus is on safety and responsibility (non-losses). These foci regulate the effects one is exposed to during the decision-making process, thus determining the way one achieves a particular goal. There exists a dominant or chronic regulatory focus and a temporary regulatory focus that can be brought upon by introducing certain stimuli (priming). Priming is an effect wherein exposure to a particular stimulus influences how one reacts to a later stimulus. Previous research involving regulatory focus and financial decision-making involved primed states of regulatory focus and established that certain assets are associated with particular regulatory foci. However, as consumers tend to make financial decisions prior to priming, this book studies how consumers' chronic regulatory focus affects financial decision-making. In this book, financial decision-making was modelled by the selection of assets and portfolios. Two main hypotheses are thus advanced. Hypothesis 1 tests whether chronic regulatory focus affects asset selection; whether chronic promotion and prevention participants select promotion and prevention assets, respectively. Hypothesis 2 tests whether chronic regulatory focus affects portfolio selection; whether chronic promotion and prevention participants select promotion and prevention portfolios, respectively. In addition, gender (Hα), age (Hβ) and education (Hγ) are associated with financial decisions; further hypotheses are advanced to explore whether these are related to asset and portfolio selection and regulatory focus.

Two complementary instruments, the eye tracker and self-report, were used to explore the hypotheses. The use of two measures is proposed to limit social desirability bias, especially since the eye tracker is an objective instrument. Participants were shown the asset selections, followed by the portfolio selections on the eye tracker, then were given the same allocation scenarios on the self-report. Participants who spent a greater proportion of time looking at a particular asset or portfolio thus indicated their selection/preference on the eye tracker. For the self-report, participants made their selection in the space provided.

The results indicated that the main hypotheses were not supported. Most participants selected the prevention asset on either measure and did not choose portfolios in accordance with their foci. Overall, chronic regulatory focus does not cause participants to select/prefer assets or portfolios that are associated with their regulatory foci. Hα and Hγ were supported indicating that gender and education are associated with regulatory focus and asset and portfolio allocation. Results indicate that females are less likely to select a prevention portfolio, but the relationship is weaker for those with a chronic prevention focus. Those who are chronic prevention-focused and possess a higher degree are more likely to look at the prevention portfolio for a proportionately longer time. Hβ was unsupported, indicating that age may not be related to regulatory focus and financial decision-making.

It is proposed that the main hypotheses were unsupported as participants were influenced by the effect of the unfavourable world financial climate, overriding the effect of their chronic regulatory focus. Seminal priming studies are currently facing issues regarding replicability, and this book postulates that events such as financial crises may be causing this effect. The eye-tracker results indicated that while participants may look at certain assets or portfolios for a proportionately longer time, they may not select it on the self-report. The eye tracker is purported to give insights into the type of information viewed by consumers but does not provide clear indication of whether this information was used to make an associated financial decision. The book then provides some avenues for future research.

Contents

List of Tables

Chapter 1
Introduction

Abstract This chapter outlines the structure of the study.

Traditional finance theory is drawn from the belief that all market participants are completely rational and calculating. However, given the recent unexpected financial crises, the inherent risks in relying too heavily on contemporary financial theory as the basis for policy discussion is inherently risky, as these theories are only suitable for problems that can be answered with scientific accuracy.

In the last decade, contemporary financial theory has come under severe criticism. Whilst it was once believed that patterns of past price behaviour will tend to recur in the future (Fama 1965), the rise of behavioural economics meant that the once lauded efficiency of the market has now made way for behavioural explanations such as herd behaviour and mass psychology (Nocera 2009). Some may believe that the environment in which the markets exist has altered, but this is not the case. People have always been irrational, contributing to market inefficiency (Fisher 2010). The only thing that has altered is that there is more focus on market participants. Thus, if financial theory is to grow and develop, researchers have to adapt to the more unpredictable and less tangible aspects of market reality.

Although financial theory has made headway into explaining stock market anomalies,[1] it has not attempted to explore the motivations behind these decisions. Without comprehending these motivations, the phenomena in question will only be observed and documented, never truly explained or understood. Delving into the motivations behind financial decisions may help in understanding how financial crises, driven by inexplicable market choices, come about. This book thus attempts to model the financial choices made by individual market participants to gain a deeper understanding into financial decision-making.

As indicated, this book aims to explore how individuals make financial decisions. One's asset and portfolio[2] allocation decisions were used to proxy for financial decisions. These model the day-to-day financial allocation decisions made by consumers. A psychological approach, *regulatory focus theory*, is used to explain these

[1]Behavioural finance, explained in Sect. 2.1.

[2]Portfolios denote a collection of investments, with its own risk/return profile, held by a company, financial institution or individual.

N. Kumar, *Chronic Regulatory Focus and Financial Decision-Making*,
SpringerBriefs in Finance, DOI 10.1007/978-981-287-694-2_1

allocation decisions. Regulatory focus theory explores the relationship between one's motivation and means of goal pursuit (Higgins 2000). It states that individuals have a dominant regulatory focus, either promotion or prevention. This dominant focus is known as chronic regulatory focus. People with different chronic regulatory foci have varying means of approaching the same goal. For example, a promotion-focused individual who wants to do well on a quiz would study hard at the library, and a prevention-focused individual would turn down an invitation to go out drinking with friends the night before (Crowe and Higgins 1997). Regulatory focus guides decision-making, and affects financial allocation decisions (Scholer et al. 2004), modelled in this book by asset and portfolio allocation decisions. In previous studies, respondents were primed[3] and their asset and account decisions were recorded (Zhou and Pham 2004). In reality, consumers do not make personal investment choices after being primed, and their chronic regulatory focus would be more of an influence. As such, this book hopes to explore how chronic regulatory focus affects asset and portfolio allocation decisions, giving rise to the research question:

Does chronic regulatory focus affect asset and portfolio allocation decisions?

The research objective of this book is to explore the relationship between chronic regulatory focus and asset and portfolio allocation:

To investigate the effect of chronic regulatory focus on asset and portfolio allocation decisions.

To measure the association between chronic regulatory focus and allocation decisions (asset and portfolio), two measures were employed; a behavioural measure using the eye tracker and self-report, using a questionnaire. Two measures were utilised to reduce the likelihood of spurious results (see Sect. 3.2) (Podsakoff et al. 2003). Utilising the eye tracker to collect behavioural data may also provide deeper understanding into how individuals make their asset and portfolio allocation decisions, primarily because the former can capture visual behaviour prior to decision-making, possibly recording subconscious behaviour (Strandvall 2013; Yarbus and Riggs 1967). The following section illustrates the significance of the research, focusing on the theoretical and practical implications of this book.

1.1 Significance

1.1.1 Theory

From a financial perspective, there has been limited research involving regulatory focus theory (Zhou and Pham 2004) or eye tracking (Shavit et al. 2010). Thus, this book hopes to deepen existing understanding in the fields of finance, consumer behaviour and eye tracking.

---

[3]Priming is an implicit memory effect in which exposure to a certain stimulus influences a response to a later stimulus.

1.1.2 *Corporations*

This book may be of use for the private sector, specifically financial institutions. Research indicates that certain financial products are sensitive to regulatory foci (Zhou and Pham 2004). By classifying customers based on their chronic regulatory focus, banks will be able to market products tailored specifically to the customers' regulatory foci. In addition, when banks are aware of the chronic regulatory foci of their clients, they may be better able to create portfolios that reduce their clients' perceived risk.

1.1.3 *Consumer Education*

1.1.3.1 Public

Once it is understood how chronic regulatory focus guides one to particular financial decisions, governments will be able to craft policy decisions that specifically cater to these foci. For example, in implementing financial literacy programs, policymakers can design versions of these programs for those of differing foci, ensuring effectiveness.

1.1.3.2 Participants

This book may benefit participants involved. They can have a greater understanding of the subconscious processes that underlie their own decision-making processes. With this knowledge, they may be able to construct less risky portfolios, not giving into their own inherent biases. In addition, the participants in this book will be able to find out their chronic regulatory focus, and thus made more aware of how they make the different decisions in their lives.

Table 1.1 Structure of book

Chapter	Title
1.0	Introduction
2.0	Literature review
3.0	Theoretical framework
4.0	Research methodology
5.0	Results
6.0	General discussion
7.0	Conclusion

1.2 Structure of Study

A detailed literature review follows, which builds the theory underpinning the study detailed in this book and outlines the process and development of the hypotheses, along with a methodology section. The results, discussion and conclusion chapters end this book. Table 1.1, briefly indicates the structure of this book.

Chapter 2
Literature Review

Abstract This chapter provides the background for the book. The chapter begins with a brief overview of behavioural finance, covering the aspects of portfolio construction, investor segmentation and securities markets. A section on prospect theory and its relevance to financial theory ends the section on behavioural finance. Further, the key concepts of regulatory focus theory were explored. The chapter concludes with a summary and critical evaluation of studies coupling both regulatory focus theory and financial concepts.

2.1 Behavioural Finance

At present, financial theory is in flux, as previously established models are being challenged and re-evaluated. Even the Markowitz Model (Markowitz 1959), the foundation of classical finance, has been called into question. Simply put, the belief that investors are rational and make cogent decisions is no longer a given, and this has called several well-established theories into question. With the vestigial effects of the subprime crisis and the ongoing European sovereign debt crisis, it is more apparent now than ever that irrational decision-making is the prime mover behind critical economic events.

Whenever the finance industry is portrayed in the media, the image that is construed is of people engaged in activity, busy in the trading room, or in their high-powered offices on Wall Street. This is a stark contrast from standard finance textbooks and early finance journals which seem to be devoid of human activity and interaction. There is much time spent on calculating rates of return, present values as such, and far too few studies on the people who are actually involved in financial markets. We all know that people are the raison d'être of financial markets, but why have they been largely ignored? Perhaps almost a century of stock price data on COMPUSTAT is hard to resist, compared to relatively few studies on the behaviour

N. Kumar, *Chronic Regulatory Focus and Financial Decision-Making*,
SpringerBriefs in Finance, DOI 10.1007/978-981-287-694-2_2

of individuals. Bluntly, if stock prices can fall 20 % in one day,[1] without any news, can one say with certainty that why people are irrelevant (Thaler 1993)?

Standard finance, also known as Modern Portfolio Theory (MPT) (Markowitz 1952), but not very modern at this point, has four foundational blocks, and posits that investors are rational, markets are efficient, investors should design their portfolios according to the rules of mean–variance portfolio theory and that expected returns are solely a function of risk (Kahneman and Tversky 1979; Statman 2008). Behavioural finance, however, restructures and questions this framework, postulating that markets are inefficient, and that investors are 'normal'. Rational investors always prefer more wealth to less, but normal ones are affected by cognitive biases and emotions (Statman 2008). Behavioural finance[2] utilises insights from the field of psychology and applies them to explain stock market anomalies and other financial issues. This may lead some to believe that behavioural finance aims to bring psychology into finance, but psychology has always been a part of finance, albeit unnoticed. Although psychological methods have been utilised to explain financial anomalies, the motivations behind these phenomena have yet to be explored. Regulatory focus theory, a goal-pursuit theory has been put forth to explain the motivations that underlie financial decisions, and will be detailed in Sect. 2.2.

The following sections will explore the various facets of behavioural finance, from portfolio construction to investor optimism, and from IPO market behaviour to dividend policy. These sections summarise the key findings in behavioural finance, to give insight into various market phenomena that exist.

2.1.1 Portfolio Construction

The simplicity of the Mean–Variance (MV) model posited in MPT suggests that it should be a relatively easy task for the average investor to create a reasonably efficient portfolio over a long-term horizon. However, behavioural finance suggests otherwise with the investor performing poorly over a long period. As per MPT, investors are supposed to maximise portfolio expected return for a given amount of risk, or equivalently minimise risk for a given level of expected return (Markowitz 1952), but this rarely occurs in reality. Instead, investors seem to do everything else but that (sentence incomplete). For example, they are more comfortable with focusing their portfolios on the assets, for example, domestic assets and their employer's stocks, regardless of whether this may increase the overall risk of the investment portfolio (Huberman 2001).

---

[1]On 19 October 1987, the Dow Jones Industrial Average dropped by 508 points to 1738.74, a 22.61 % change.

[2]Behavioural finance is the use of psychological methods to explain the behaviour of investors and subsequent market effects (Sewell 2010).

The above phenomenon is known as home bias,[3] resulting in a focus on domestic securities despite, the possible reduction in risk by international diversification (Tesar and Werner 1995). Investors in more patriotic nations hold smaller amounts of international equities (Morse and Shive 2011), very different from the predictions of asset pricing models, which state that investors should hold the world market portfolio of all countries in proportion to each country's market capitalisation. Home bias is extensive across countries (Chkioua and Abaoub 2012), although varying greatly in effect (Solnik and Zuo 2012), and has fallen in recent years (Foad 2012). Several reasons have been put forward, such as a desire to hedge domestic inflation, but such an explanation does not yield as equities do not hedge inflation in such a way, given the investment horizon of most portfolios. Other explanations, such as investors being more optimistic about local equities than compared to foreign investors (French and Poterba 1991) or the existence of international boundaries resulting in exchange risk, etc. (Ke et al. 2009) have been put forward, but these are hard to model, and thus far not proven conclusively, similar to other investor idiosyncrasies.

Overconfidence is also a key factor in constructing portfolios, wherein investors, whilst aware of the benefits of diversification, hold under-diversified portfolios due to an illusory sense of control which makes them adopt naive diversification strategies (Goetzmann and Kumar 2001). Overconfidence explains much in the area of portfolio selection, such as why portfolio managers trade so much and why pension funds hire active equity managers, all strategies that are inconsistent with notions of rationality (Thaler and Bondt 1995).

2.1.2 Investor Segmentation

Several studies have been conducted in regard to categorising investors into various subgroups, based on financial knowledge, allocation strategies and personality, (Bailard et al. 1986; Gunnarsson and Wahlund 1997; Harrison 1994; Pompian 2012; Waneryd 2001; Wood and Zaichkowsky 2004) instead of treating them as a homogeneous and wholly rational unit, as done by MPT. Keller and Siegrist (2006) divided investors into 'Safe Players', 'Open Books', 'Money Dummies' and 'Risk Seekers', by virtue of their risk attitudes and perceptions toward securities, the stock market and gambling. Age is also found to be a causal factor in risk aversion (Riley and Chow 1992), along with one's occupation, wherein corporate executives and lawyers are found to be more risk averse (Barnewall 1987) and even the Myers–Briggs Type Indicator (MBTI) has been used to segment investors (Filbeck et al. 2005). Gender yields differences as well, with female investors exhibiting more risk aversion than male investors (Barsky et al. 1997). Unlike classical finance,

[3]Home bias refers to the tendency of investors to invest in a large and disproportionate amount of domestic equities, relative to their overall portfolio.

behavioural finance does not view investors as having the same standardised and rational goals, instead construing the former as unique segments with varying and sometimes opposing aims.

2.1.3 Securities Markets

The capstone of capital markets research theorises that it is not possible to consistently achieve above average market returns, given the current information. This is more formally defined as the Efficient Market Hypothesis (EMH), which has three major forms, 'weak', 'semi-strong' and 'strong'. This theory, developed in the 1960s (Fama 1965; Samuelson 1965), state that when faced with new information some investors may underreact and others may overreact with an overall random pattern that conforms to a normal distribution. This results in a situation wherein market prices cannot be reliably exploited to make abnormal profits. Some of the classical finance thread espouses the maxim that the best established fact in economics is the efficiency of securities markets (Jensen 1978). However, many feel, especially in the aftermath of the recent financial crisis, that the blind trust in such a framework (Volcker 2011) along with deregulation, such as the Gramm–Leach–Biley Act,[4] has led to the downward spiral of the global economy. Brusquely put by Shiller (1981), the failure of the efficient market model is so dramatic, that it would seem impossible to attribute the failure to such things as data errors, price index problems or changes in tax laws. Behavioural finance sees the flaws in financial markets as due to cognitive biases and human error, as outlined below.

Investor sentiment, defined as the belief about future cash flows and investment risks that are not justified by the facts available (Baker and Wurgler 2007), is one of the central tenets of behavioural finance. This phenomenon proposes to explain sudden swings in the markets, for example, the rise and fall of internet stocks in the 1990s (Baker and Wurgler 2013). Baker and Wurgler (2007) have shown that it is possible to measure investor sentiment, creating indices of the latter for the global markets and find that it plays a critical role in international market volatility (Baker et al. 2012).

Investors irrationally hold on to losing stocks, known as the disposition effect,[5] possibly to avoid confronting their incorrect investment decisions (Hirshleifer 2001; Shefrin and Statman 1985). This effect can cause underreaction to news, leading to

---

[4]The Gramm-Leach-Biley Act repealed part of the Glass-Steagall Act of 1933, removing market barriers among banks, securities and insurance companies that prohibited any one institution from acting as both an investment bank, commercial bank or insurance company. With the Gramm-Leach-Biley Act, consolidation was allowed. Thus, people were then able to invest and save at the same financial institution.

[5]The disposition effect is the tendency of investors to sell shares whose price has increased, while keeping those that have dropped in value.

predictable returns and post-announcement price drift[6] (Frazzini 2006). The disposition effect is highest in non-professional and low-income investors (Dhar and Zhu 2002), reflecting that investors cannot be thought of a single and rational unit.

There exists the momentum effect, where past winners almost always outperform past losers (Jegadeesh and Titman 2001b). Stocks that perform the best or worst over a 3–12 months period tend to continue to perform well or poorly respectively over the subsequent 3–12 months (Jegadeesh and Titman 1993). Under the EMH, any predictable patterns in return should be swiftly eliminated. However, momentum profits have been found in most major developed markets in the world, excluding Japan (Jegadeesh and Titman 2001a). Whilst returns appear to exhibit momentum in the short–medium run, they tend to revert to fundamentals in the long run (Hong and Stein 1999).

Specifically concerning the internet boom, investor sentiment played a major role in the stock prices of firms. Those that dropped the 'dotcom' naming conventions to dissociate themselves from the internet sector after the price crash saw a positive announcement effect (Cooper et al. 2005). It thus appears that the effect of investor sentiment is so severe that it can cause price variations even from manifestations as trite as company name changes.

Research has shown that certain times of the year, in this case, January, predicate certain feelings in stock market investors, with the market performing well overall and smaller stocks out-performing larger ones (Anderson et al. 2007; Keim 1983; Rozeff and Kinney 1976). January is viewed to be one month of renewed optimism, with investors, regardless of their failure in that year, concluding that they can correct their mistakes on the next attempt, resulting in a perpetual January Effect cycle (Ciccone 2011; Polivy and Herman 2002). There is also evidence that it is the risk premium and not the risk itself that is higher in January, perhaps indicating that the January effect is due to higher compensation for risk in that month, rather than due to just risk (Sun and Tong 2010). The fact that disappointed investors never seem to learn, and mitigate that the cycle is testament to their irrationality, running against the grain of the everrational investors in the MPT sphere. Recent findings also indicate that the January effect is weakening (Jones and Pomorski 2002), but it is unclear whether this means that investors are becoming more rational, or some other effect is at play.

Notwithstanding monthly effects, even different days of the week predicate varying effects in the market, with the highest returns on Wednesday, and the lowest on Monday (Berument and Kiymaz 2001) and with the highest selling activity on the present day (Abraham and Ikenberry 1994). Also, Friday's returns are lower when Saturday is a trading day (Keim and Stambaugh 1983), with little reasonable explanation (Gibbons and Hess 1981), and the last trading day before holidays exhibits abnormally high returns (Ariel 1990; Kim and Park 1994). Returns from the May–October period are lower than the remainder of the year,

[6]The post-announcement price drift is the tendency for a stock's cumulative abnormal returns to move in a direction that will yield results that are higher or lower than analysts' predictions.

known as the 'Halloween Indicator' and are often negative, but no explanation has been posited for this effect thus far (Bouman and Jacobsen 2002).

Even lunar phases have an effect on the stock market, with lower returns on days around a full moon than compared to those around a new moon (Floros and Tan 2013; Yuan et al. 2006). This has been observed for all the major U.S. stock indexes, and several other countries, but with no effects on return volatility or trading volume (Dichev and Janes 2003). Such effects are impossible to reconcile with rational means of price setting, and are clearly in opposition to all forms of the efficient markets hypothesis.

The weather affects markets as well; sunshine is positively correlated with stock returns (Dowling and Lucey 2005; Hirshleifer and Shumway 2003). The weather in New York City is has a long history of significant correlation with major stock indexes (Saunders 1993), completely unjustifiable by the MPT. Geomagnetic storms, during their recovery phase, also appear to negatively affect several international stock indices, with a more pronounced effect for smaller capitalisation stocks, perhaps due to the profound effect on people's moods and that small capitalisation stocks are generally held by individuals, who are likely to be more affected by mood than institutional investors (Krivelyova and Robotti 2003).

Sports results also affect market returns, with losses in international soccer matches having negative effects on global stock markets (Edmans et al. 2007). There also exists the Super Bowl Stock Market Predictor,[7] which if used as an investment strategy, over the 1967–1988 period, yields higher returns than a buy and hold strategy over the same period, clearly inconsistent with the efficient markets hypothesis (Krueger and Kennedy 1990). The Super Bowl also has other effects, with abnormal buying activity amongst small traders for recognised Super Bowl advertisers' shares (Fehle et al. 2005).

In relation to stock market data, it is found that despite investors acquiring useful information, they somehow misinterpret it and underperform the market (Barber and Odean 2000; Odean 1999). The type of audience to which the information is presented, is also significant. Unsophisticated investors[8] assess a firm's earnings performance to be higher when presented with more positive pro-forma earnings prior to Generally Accepted Accounting Principles (GAAP) earnings, than compared to when only shown GAAP earnings. Sophisticated investors, however, were not affected by the order of presentation or the information presented (Elliot 2006; Victoravich 2010).

In the perfect markets imagined by Miller and Modigliani, dividend policy is inconsequential to a firm's value, and stockholders should complain if a firm pays

---

[7]The Super Bowl Stock Market Predictor indicates that, if the Super Bowl is won by a team from the old National Football League, the stock market will finish the year higher than it began (Stovall, 1989). However, if the game is won by a team from the old American Football League, the market will finish lower than it began.

[8]Sophisticated investors are those who possess stock market investment experience, and knowledge acquired through this experience and other practices, such as, completion of finance and accounting courses and certifications.

tax dividends, given that dividends are taxed at a higher rate than capital gains. However, stockholders often do the opposite, complaining when dividends are cut (Thaler and Bondt 1995). This illogical mode of thought may be because investors psychologically resist utilising their capital and view dividends as a separate gain when the stock price rises, and a fall back for price drops (Shefrin and Statman 1984). Repeatedly, the axioms of conventional finance have been challenged by contemporary financial phenomena.

Fashions and fads also affect securities prices, especially since investors are influenced by their social environment and are pressured to conform (Aronson 1991). For example, a downtrend may occur during a financial crisis, when investors irrationally decide to unload their holdings, as per the actions of their neighbour, or when a market guru prescribes the latest stock or investment heuristic. Investors face an uphill task when it comes to selecting securities, given the staggering amounts available. As most investors do not have access to a retail broker to suggest what they should purchase, they end up buying what is discussed in the media, those which have performed unusually well or poorly (Odean 1999).

The above phenomena could be explained by herding,[9] which may also have led to bank panics, when depositors run on banks, seeing other depositors proceeding as such. Several herding models exist (Brunnermeier 2001), and there are higher levels of herding in small stocks (Wermers 1999). Furthermore, stocks bought by herds have higher returns than those sold by herds (Wermers 1999). Analysts release earnings forecasts that do not vary much from prior expectations, with a tendency to report forecasts similar to those released by other analysts, although their private information may justify differing forecasts (Trueman 1994).

Age also appears to play a part, as younger analysts are more prone to herding than their older contemporaries, with the former forecasting closer to the consensus forecast (Hong et al. 2000). It is observed that the twin stock of multinational companies, with nearly identical cash flows, move more like the markets where they trade most intensively than otherwise expected (Froot and Dabora 1999). This is in opposition to the classical finance paradigm that predicts that an asset's price is unaffected by its trade location.

Although behavioural finance is unable to resolve all the conundrums that exist within finance, it has done an admirable job of attempting to explain some of the ever irrational behaviour of investors, by passing every boom and bust. Whilst trading frequency seems to eliminate some market anomalies (Dhar and Zhu 2002; List 2003), perennial issues such as the Closed-End Fund Puzzle[10] and Equity Premium Puzzle[11] (Mehra and Prescott 1985) are still unresolved, although insights

[9]Herding can be defined as behaviour patterns that are correlated across individuals.

[10]Since closed-end funds are exchange traded, their prices are different from the net asset value, defined as the closed-end fund puzzle.

[11]The equity premium puzzle stems from the fact that the demand for government bonds is high, despite the fact that they return less than stocks, and why there is even a demand at all.

have been provided by the mechanisms of behavioural finance (Bernartzi and Thaler 1995; Lee et al. 1991). The overarching aim of behavioural finance is then not to replace the methods that compose classical finance, but to explain market anomalies, and complement existing frameworks that are already in place.

As a whole, behavioural finance explores how investors act in given situations, and attempts to explain market anomalies. However, the means by which one pursues such goals is yet unexplored. Delving into the means of goal pursuit are necessary to understand how and why participants move toward these goals. Without comprehending these means, the market effects observed in behavioural finance will only be observed, never truly understood. Failing to grasp the means and underlying motivations of these behaviours, policies implemented to prevent future financial crises which are unlikely to be effective. Regulatory focus theory, as described in the following section, is putforth to explain the relationship between one's motivations and the associated goal.

2.2 Regulatory Focus Theory

Behavioural finance takes into account the behaviour of investors, in particular their irrationality and biases, but fails to consider the association between one's motivation and the ways in which they achieve various goals. Since financial decisions, represented in this book by asset and portfolio allocation scenarios, are made to achieve goals that are distant in time, these choices are likely to be directed by the processes known as self-regulation (Zhou and Pham 2004). Self-regulation is defined as the process that individuals utilise to set their goals, pick means to accomplish these goals and assess progress toward the latter (Carver and Scheier 1998).

Regulatory focus theory states that self-regulation involves two differing systems, promotion and prevention (Higgins 2000). The promotion system, derived from the regulation of nurturance needs, relies on approach strategies whilstregulating toward desirable ends, whereas the prevention system, derived from the regulation of security needs, relies on avoidance strategies whilstregulating toward desirable ends. The promotion system is thus active under the pursuit of ideals, defined as the pursuit of wishes, dreams and aspirations, whilst the prevention system is active under the pursuit of 'oughts', defined as the fulfilment of responsibilities, obligations and duties (Higgins 2000).

Promotion self-regulation is concerned with approaching matches in a desired state, and prevention self-regulation is concerned with avoiding mismatches in a desired state (Florack et al. 2010). For example, to keep a slim figure, a promotion-focused individual would be more likely to exercise (approach a match), whereas a prevention-focused individual would be more likely to avoid eating fatty foods (avoid a mismatch) (Florack et al. 2010). In financial context, with goal being to maximise wealth, a promotion-focused individual would be more likely to invest in stock (approach risk), whilst a prevention-focused individual would be more likely to invest in a mutual fund (avoid risk) (Zhou and Pham 2004). Thus, promotion and prevention-focused individuals differ in their strategic inclinations when approaching a desired goal.

In order to comprehend regulatory focus theory, it is necessary to understand regulatory fit theory. Regulatory fit is defined as the increased motivation intensity that results when there is a match between the manner in which a person pursues a goal and their goal orientation (Aaker and Lee 2006). People experience regulatory fit when the manner of their engagement in an activity sustains, instead of disrupting, their current motivational orientation or interests (Higgins 2000). Fit makes people engage more strongly in what they are doing and feel right about it, and individuals can thus pursue the same goal with different orientations and ways (Higgins 2005), as highlighted in the preceding paragraph. Fit influences the strength of value experiences and perceived success (Freitas and Higgins 2002), independent of the pain or pleasure felt with such outcomes. Thus, when people pursue a goal that is in accordance with their orientation, they experience their engagement in that goal pursuit more strongly than if they were to pursue the goal at odds with their orientation, with regulatory fit making one feel right about their reactions to situations (Freitas and Higgins 2002). As such, poor regulatory fit or non-fit would result if the incorrect type or level of means is utilised, for example, vigilance avoidance means for goal pursuit in a promotion focus or low vigilance during goal pursuit in a prevention focus respectively (Higgins 2002). When a situation has a fit with one's regulatory focus, it is often viewed as being more right, regardless of one's mood or the manner of the situation (Camacho et al. 2003).

Chronic regulatory focus is the dominant regulatory focus of a person. Whilst both the promotion and prevention systems are perceived to coexist in every person, one or the other may be made temporarily more accessible (momentary regulatory focus) (Higgins 1998). Momentary regulatory focus is achieved by differing methods such as priming or framing. These are techniques used to make the prevention or promotion systems temporarily more dominant. The promotion system can be made momentarily more accessible by priming a person's ideals (Higgins et al. 1994; Pham and Avnet 2004), or by framing a task in an approach manner (Roney et al. 1995), while the prevention system can be made more accessible by priming a person's oughts, or by framing a task in an avoidance manner. Priming can be achieved by asking participants to describe how their current ideals or oughts changed as they grew up (Higgins et al. 1994; Liberman et al. 1999). For the promotion condition, participants could be asked to list down their current hopes and goals, and how they varied from those during their childhood. For the prevention condition, participants could be asked to write down their current duties and obligations, and how they differed from those during their childhood (Lin and Shen 2012). Framing is achieved by instructing participants to complete a paper-and-pencil maze, featuring a mouse with either a piece of cheese at the entrance or predatory owl looming over the maze (Friedman and Förster 2001). In the promotion condition, participants were instructed to guide the mouse to the cheese to seek nurturance, and in the prevention condition, to guide the mouse to safety, away from the owl.

People with a promotion focus tend to use eagerness as a means to accomplish promotion-focused outcomes, and those with a prevention focus use vigilance means to achieve prevention-focused outcomes (Higgins 2002). More specifically, those in an eagerness state from a promotion focus should want to achieve 'hits' and avoid errors of omission, and those in a state of vigilance from a prevention focus should want to accomplish correct rejections (Crowe and Higgins 1997), thus promotion is interested in gaining additions, and prevention is concerned in preventing subtractions (Roese et al. 1999).

Culture also plays a part, as the promotion system is more chronically accessible for people from individualist cultures, and the prevention system is more accessible for people from collectivist cultures (Lee et al. 2000). This is unsurprising as differences in how the self is defined, how relationships with others are imagined and what values are consistent within an individualism and collectivism framework (Oyserman and Lee 2008), and not less for chronic regulatory focus. Those with strong and accessible ideals, and those with strong and accessible oughts, have greater chronic access to their promotion and prevention systems, respectively (Higgins et al. 1986).

Compared to prevention-focused individuals, promotion-focused individuals tend to be more willing to accept new options and courses of action, more willing to take investment risks and more likely to rely on emotions and existing biases. Prevention-focused individuals tend to prefer status quo options and make investments that are more conservative and are more disbelieving of manipulative persuasion attempts (Kirmani and Zhu 2007). In general, promotion-focused individuals strive for matches to their goals, thus they are in a state of eagerness to include as many options as possible to achieve these goals. Preventionfocused individuals however, concentrate on avoiding mismatches to their goals, leading them to be in a state of vigilance, where they contemplate upon, more restrictively, only clearly apt choices (Zhu and Meyers-Levy 2007). Promotionfocused individuals tend to maximise hits and reduce misses, prevention-focused individuals tend to maximise correct rejections and minimise false alarms. Promotion-focused individuals also emphasise speed over accuracy, with prevention-focused individuals doing the reverse (Pham and Chang 2010). Given its roots in one's motivation systems, regulatory focus has been applied to a large variety of domains. The paragraphs that follow illustrate how regulatory focus has explained behaviour across various fields.

2.2.1 *Creativity*

The capacity for creativity has been studied from a regulatory focus perspective. Promotion-focused individuals were able to generate more original ideas and evaluate the originality of their ideas more accurately, than compared to prevention-focused individuals (Friedman and Förster 2001; Herman and Reiter-Palmon 2011; Lam and Chiu 2002). However, while a promotion focus is beneficial for evaluating originality, it is unfavourable for evaluating quality, with the reverse for a prevention focus (Herman and Reiter-Palmon 2011).

2.2.2 *Coaching*

In a global company, when a coach's coaching orientation matched that of the recipients, there was a more positive effect on the latter (Chan 2012). Even different structures in an organisation have a better fit with tasks of a certain regulatory focus (Dimotakis 2012). Studies also demonstrate that a prevention focus, be it momentary or chronic, compared to a promotion focus, leads one to copy the management behaviour of a role model, regardless of how one felt about this behaviour earlier, as its recipient (Zhang et al. 2011).

2.2.3 *Impression Management and Reputation*

There also exists a relationship between regulatory focus and exemplification or supplication impression management techniques—the want to regulate how others view us. The prevention focus and exemplification tactics are related, along with the promotion focus and exemplification and supplication (Kacmar and Tucker 2014). Behavioural integrity reinforces the association between the prevention (promotion) focus and exemplification (supplication), but not with the promotion focus and exemplification. There exists a positive association between levels of prevention focus and reputational issues such as those outside the Big Five and perceived stress (Pfattheicher 2015). Prevention-oriented individuals are also more likely to donate money when they are exposed to reputation cues, independent of the Big Five.

2.2.4 *Romantic Relationships*

Promotion-focused individuals approached their partners more often, observed higher partner responsiveness and more support when discussing less achievable promotion-oriented goals. Low-partner responsiveness with promotion-aligned goals was associated with higher self-efficacy, for promotion-focused individuals (Winterheld and Simpson 2015). Prevention-focused people observed more responsiveness with less distanced partners, whilst prevention related goals were discussed (Winterheld and Simpson 2015). Thus, it appears that regulatory focus manages the interaction of individuals and their relationship environment with respect to motivational needs.

2.2.5 *Coping at Work*

Hotel employees who were promotion-focused were more likely to task-cope, whereas prevention-focused employees were less likely to emotion- and avoidance-cope (Jung and Yoon 2015). Thus, it appears that regulatory focus has an important role to play in employee behaviour, much like other factors, such as personality or values.

2.2.6 *Information Processing*

When people are unmotivated to process information, they tend to rely on their regulatory focus to filter out information that they deem irrelevant. Those who are promotion-focused selectively pay attention to benefits that address nurturance concerns, and prevention-focused individuals selectively pay attention to benefits that address safety and security concerns (Wang and Lee 2006). Information is also recalled better when it is consistent with self-regulatory goals (Aaker and Lee 2001).

Regulatory focus theory is linked to the way messages are perceived (Kirmani and Zhu 2007). When presented with ambiguous ad claims, prevention-focused participants perceive these claims to be more manipulative than promotion-focused participants (Kirmani and Zhu 2007). When individuals' regulatory orientations were compatible with the product attributes emphasised in the ad, the messages in the ad were more persuasive, than when it was not (Latimer et al. 2008; Lin and Shen 2012; Zhao and Pechmann 2007). Promotion-focused individuals found that messages were more persuasive when hedonic[12] attributes were emphasised, and prevention-focused individuals found messages with utilitarian attributes more convincing (Chernev 2004). In regard to brand evaluations, when promotion-focused individuals viewed hedonic attributes framed as gains, and prevention-focused individuals viewed utilitarian attributes framed as losses, results were more favourable (Lin and Shen 2012).

---

[12]When a product is described as 'hedonic' it means that its purpose is to bring pleasure, fun and excitement to the user, in comparison to a 'utilitarian' product, which is primarily instrumental, and its purchase would be motivated by functional product aspects (Khan et al. 2005).

Concerning deal sites such as Groupon and Living Social, the matching of regulatory focus appears to bolster the persuasiveness of the messages (Pentina and Taylor 2013). Varying mechanisms operate for each foci; prevention-oriented consumers centrally process offers which are representative of either foci, unlike their promotion-focused counterparts. Also, when individuals make judgements for distant persons, they are more influenced by promotion-framed adverts, although no differential framing effects on judgements of proximal entities exists (Park and Morton 2015).

2.2.7 *Decision Making*

2.2.7.1 General Decision Making

Decision makers in a promotion focus will view promotion-focused outcomes as more important in their decision than prevention-focused outcomes, and the same goes for prevention-focused decision makers (Higgins 2002). When people make choices for others or themselves, a different regulatory focus is dominant. In general, those who make decisions for others, or proxy decision makers, they examine and seek out more information than those who make their own choices, or personal decision makers (Jonas et al. 2005; Kray 2000; Polman 2010; Polman and Emich 2011). Among personal decision makers, a prevention focus is activated, and among proxy decision makers, a promotion focus is activated (Polman 2012).

Even the willingness of participants to continue working on tasks is affected by their chronic regulatory focus (Wan et al. 2009). In an experiment, participants were interrupted whilst in the process of describing an abstract figure, then given a choice after the interruption to resume describing the same figure or alternatively, switching to the task of describing a new figure. Those with a promotion focus were more willing to switch to a new description than those with a prevention focus, who were more likely to continue to describe the same figure (Wan et al. 2009). The amount of choices available is also associated with regulatory focus. When there are more choices, the promotion focus leads to increases in choice confidence and likelihood (Som and Lee 2012).

2.2.7.2 Economic Decision Making

The chronic orientation, in tandem with the way a product is chosen, has an effect on the monetary value of the latter (Avnet and Higgins 2006). This may have implications for the way consumers value and select investment products. In an experiment conducted by Avnet and Higgins (2006), where participants were given a choice between two varieties of the same product, chronic promotion-focused participants' use of emotions to make a choice which increased the monetary value of the chosen product, whilst chronic prevention-focused participants' use of emotions to make a choice having the opposite effect. When prevention-focused participants used reason to make a choice, the monetary value of the product increased, with the reverse effect for promotion-focused participants.

Participants in the feeling-based condition were told to rate for several pre-selected emotions when exposed to the products and those in the reason-based condition were told to rate their evaluation of each product for pre-determined evaluation items. Promotion-focused people who received success feedback experience fit and prevention-focused people experienced non-fit, whereas prevention-focused people who received failure feedback experience fit and promotion-oriented people experienced non-fit (Avnet and Higgins 2006). Regarding retail shopping, the promotion (prevention) focus is positively (negatively) associated with impulsiveness (Das 2015). The promotion (prevention) focus also has a negative (positive) relationship with attitudinal and behavioural loyalty.

2.2.8 Summary

Thus, regulatory focus theory is able to explain behaviour over several domains, indicating its generalisability. In this regard, the next section explores how regulatory focus can be applied to finance. However, solely applying regulatory focus theory to research regarding financial decision-making is inadequate. This book thus applies both regulatory focus theory and existing financial concepts in studying financial decision-making. This will allow the study to advance an unbiased understanding of how one makes financial allocation choices, without overlooking theories that may give insight to the issue at hand.

2.3 Finance and Regulatory Focus Theory

Behavioural finance explores how investors make decisions, the use of regulatory focus theory to further comprehend the processes by which investors make these decisions and the underlying motivations behind these processes is the purported next step in the behavioural finance framework. At present, there has been limited research regarding an amalgam of regulatory focus theory and financial concepts, and this book aims to develop on existing research in this area (Zhou and Pham 2004).

The work by Zhou and Pham (2004) proposes that consumers' investment decisions involve processes of promotion and prevention regulation that are managed by varying mental accounts, with different financial products representative of promotion versus prevention orientations. It is postulated that different risk attitudes are by-products of promotion and prevention in environments where seizing opportunities and achieving gains increases risk and preventing mistakes and avoiding losses decreases risk. From a regulatory focus standpoint, the book demonstrates that promotion and prevention can be activated by the targets of judgement and decision, not only individual differences or situational factors, as with previous research.

From a financial standpoint, investors' goals may be determined by the investment opportunities underevaluation rather than being independent of these opportunities, and that the returns and risks of each financial product are evaluated separately, rather than jointly, as proposed by classical finance theory. The experiments demonstrate that priming can affect the asset and account allocation process, and that the evaluation of financial products can serve as a prime for unrelated tasks, sensitive to prevention and promotion. Whilst the bidirectional causality between priming by unrelated tasks, asset and account allocation has been highlighted, along with extensions to financial theory, the method by which chronic prevention and promotion-focused individuals approach asset and portfolio allocation is unexplored.

The study by Scholer et al. (2010) explores the self-regulatory mechanisms that underpin risk-seeking behaviour under loss, via stock investment studies. The experiments explored how participants behaved when they had purportedly lost or gained in their investment, and what they would subsequently invest in, from a range of stock options presented. It was also studied whether priming would alter the nature of stock options selected, along with whether those of varying chronic regulatory foci would make differing selections. The results were that prevention-focused individuals, more than promotion-focused ones, chose the riskier stock after an initial loss than when compared to a situation with an initial gain. When participants were primed with either a prevention or a promotion focus, it was found that the prevention-primed individuals were more risk seeking when a risky option offered the only possibility of getting to the original investment amount, but when a conservative option was available, this option was selected. There was no observable effect for a promotion prime. The study was then repeated without the prime, and there were similar results, with chronic prevention-focused participants. Across the experiments, the prevention system, but not the promotion system predicted the extent of risky decision-making. There were no significant results for the promotion focus thus indicating the possibility that the chronic prevention system is stronger in situations that involve financial decision-making. Although stock investments are featured prominently, they seem to be more of a vehicle to explore risk seeking behaviour, rather than asset allocation.

Concepts drawn from both studies would be useful for exploring the regulatory foci supporting investment decisions, as the Zhou and Pham (2004) study fails to explore how chronic regulatory focus interplays with financial choices, and Scholer et al. (2010) do not look into how different financial products and portfolios are affected by regulatory focus. Whilst behavioural finance attempts to explain various anomalies using theories from psychology and the decision sciences, there are still many modes of thought and fields of study that have not been explored, to answer the questions that are posed by finance. Prospect theory makes a distinction between various pursuing and not pursuing courses of action, but it does not take into account the motivations for goal pursuit (Idson et al. 2011), which is the aim of regulatory focus theory.

Regulatory focus theory has been applied to several fields, as diverse as politics (Boldero and Higgins 2011) and medicine (Klenk et al. 2011), extending the knowledge base in these areas. Whenever people are involved in decision-making processes, it seems that regulatory focus has a part to play, no less in finance. Thus, further study should be embarked upon, with a regulatory focus lens, pushing both areas ahead. The section that follows outlines the theoretical framework that underlies the book, drawn from the extensive literature review conducted.

Chapter 3
Theoretical Framework

Abstract This chapter begins with the development of the hypotheses, which regard the relationship between chronic regulatory focus with asset (H1) and portfolio (H2) allocation. The dependent variable (asset and portfolio allocation), independent variable (chronic regulatory focus) and the control variables (gender, age group, ethnicity, marital status, education and financial literacy) will then be reviewed. The means of measurement for these variables will then conclude the chapter.

3.1 Statement of Hypotheses

Research indicates that primed states of promotion and prevention are associated with certain assets (Zhou and Pham 2004). As primed states of regulatory focus are associated with certain assets, i.e. stock are associated with the promotion focus, and mutual funds are associated with the prevention focus, it is hypothesised that chronic regulatory focus is associated with the same assets:

H1: *Chronic regulatory focus affects asset allocation decisions; promotion and prevention-focused participants will choose promotion and prevention-based assets respectively.*

Although individuals may have preferences for and varying levels of familiarity with different assets, they would generally possess a portfolio of some form. This portfolio may include real estate, bonds and various other assets. A portfolio would thus represent most of the financial allocation decisions one would make, it buying an investment property or purchasing a bond. In order to accurately capture all forms of financial allocation decisions, both the asset and the portfolio are necessary.

N. Kumar, *Chronic Regulatory Focus and Financial Decision-Making*,
SpringerBriefs in Finance, DOI 10.1007/978-981-287-694-2_3

The portfolios in this book have their own risk/return profile and are proposed to be associated with states of promotion and prevention. Portfolio allocation is more directly reflective of the regulatory focus concept of 'promotion being interested in gaining additions, and prevention concerned with preventing subtractions' (Roese et al. 1999), than when compared to account allocation scenarios in previous research (Zhou and Pham 2004). Two portfolios have been provided for this book, one reflective of the promotion focus, and one reflective of the prevention focus, elaborated upon in Sect. 4.3.2.

Portfolios that gain in value over time, but may also lose value, and portfolios that maintain their value, accounting for inflation are proposed to be reflective of states of promotion and prevention respectively. Compared to asset allocation decisions, portfolios capture more of the day-to-day financial allocation decisions undertaken by consumers. A more realistic reflection of financial allocation decisions is necessary for effective policy-making, thus leading to the hypothesis:

H2: *Chronic regulatory focus affects portfolio allocation decisions; promotion and prevention-focused participants will choose promotion and prevention-based portfolios respectively.*

As per the results section, it is observed that both hypotheses are supported. This forms the crux of the study and will be illustrated further in the discussion. The validity of both hypotheses will be tested by the eye tracker and self-report. These, along with the variables of the study will be explained in detail in the following sections.

3.1.1 Further Hypotheses

It is known that gender (Powell and Ansic 1997), age (Chen and Sun 2003) and education (Cole et al. 2012) have an effect on financial decision-making. Given that financial decision-making is related to regulatory focus, it is possible that these variables are associated with gender, age and education. Thus, their relationship will be examined in the following additional hypotheses:

Hα: *Gender is associated with regulatory focus and asset and portfolio decisions.*

Hβ: *Age is associated with regulatory focus and asset and portfolio decisions.*

Hγ: *Education is associated with regulatory focus and asset and portfolio decisions.*

As elaborated upon in the next section, these variables will also be used as control variables in exploring the main hypotheses.

3.2 Variables

The dependent variable is the participants' allocation choices, either the asset (H1) or portfolio (H2), tested with the eye tracker and self-report (pen and paper using a questionnaire with the allocation scenarios). H1 and H2 were first assessed by the eye tracker, then the self-report. The independent variable is the participant's chronic regulatory focus. Table 3.1, as below, indicates the variables involved, their nature (dependent/independent) and means of measurement.

The data that results from the self-report may be distorted due to the human tendency to present oneself in the best possible light (Fisher 1993). The subsequent findings may be systematically biased toward respondents' perceptions of what is 'right' or socially acceptable (Maccoby and Maccoby 1954). This phenomenon is known as social desirability bias, and is pervasive across all fields (Levy 1981; Peltier and Walsh 1990). Social desirability bias can lead to common method variance,[1] which can be a potential problem in behavioural research (Podsakoff et al. 2003). Especially in the selection of assets and portfolios, participants may feel the need to choose assets that are socially acceptable for their demographic, e.g. wealthier participants may feel the need to select risky assets (Waneryd 2001). This may cause spurious results or conceal the relationship between variables in the study (Ganster et al. 1983). Most methods that propose to deal with social desirability bias involve surveys with multiple items (Nederhof 1985), irrelevant to the allocation choices in this book. Podsakoff et al. (2003) proposed that the variables could be collected from different sources to remedy the issue of social desirability bias. Thus, the eye tracker was used to provide the behavioural data regarding allocation choice, to complement the self-report. The eye tracker is an objective measure (Duchowski 2007), which when used in tandem with the self-report, will limit the possibility of the mind-set of participants to bias the relationship between the dependent and independent variables (Podsakoff et al. 2003). The use of two measures to test the hypotheses may cause loss of information if data on the independent and dependent variables are not linked (Podsakoff et al. 2003), but care was taken in the research to prevent such occurrences. Moreover, the eye tracker allows the researcher to 'step into another's shoes' and collect data from the user's point of view. This allows the researcher to obtain objective information about consumer behaviours, from the consumer's perspective (Starr and Fernandez 2007).

A Pearson chi-squared test was first conducted to determine association between allocation choice and chronic regulatory focus. Then, to gain further insight, a simple logistic regression was conducted. This model measures the relationship between a categorical dependent variable (allocation choice) and categorical independent variable (chronic regulatory focus) (Bhandari and Joensson 2009). Research has stated that gender, age group, ethnicity (Weber and Hsee 1998), marital status (Grable 2000), education and financial literacy (Rooij et al. 2007) are

[1]Common method variance is variance that is attributable to the measurement method rather than the constructs that the measures represent (Podsakoff et al. 2003).

Table 3.1 Variable list (Hypotheses)

Variables	Nature	Measure
Allocation choice (asset and portfolio)	Dependent	Eye tracker and self-report
Chronic regulatory focus	Independent	Composite regulatory focus scale

related to financial decision-making. Thus, these demographic variables were used as control variables in the logit model, to test the relative impact of chronic regulatory focus on allocation choice.

In this book, financial literacy was controlled, by selecting participants who are known to have the requisite levels of knowledge to understand the situations presented. The participants' level of financial literacy was reconfirmed with a financial literacy test, immediately after the main experiment was conducted. The result of this test was coded as the financial literacy variable in the logistic regression. This variable functions only as a control variable, and further analysis into financial literacy will not be conducted. Section 3.2.3 provides further details regarding financial literacy. The Chronic Regulatory Focus Scale, allocation choices on the self-report and financial literacy questions are on the same questionnaire provided to the participants. The sections that follow elaborate upon the measures are indicated in Table 3.1.

3.2.1 Assessment of Chronic Regulatory Focus

Chronic regulatory focus was measured by the Composite Regulatory Focus Scale (CRFS) (Haws et al. 2010) and was the first portion of the experimental design. Several other methods exist to measure chronic regulatory focus, and they will be described herein. These are the Regulatory Focus Questionnaire (RFQ), developed by Higgins (2001), the BIS/BAS Scale by Carver and White (1994) to assess the regulatory systems developed by Gray (1990), Selves Questionnaire by Higgins (1986) and the measure developed by Lockwood (2002).

The RFQ has six reflective items assessing chronic promotion and five assessing chronic prevention focus. The RFQ conceptualises promotion and prevention success using promotion and prevention pride respectively, which are anticipatory responses to new task goals derived from an individual's subjective history of promotion and prevention goal attainment success (Higgins 2002). Both the prevention and promotion sub-scales have a low correlation with each other, indicating independence (Haws et al. 2010).

Carver and White (1994) developed the BIS/BAS scale to assess Gray's (1990) regulatory systems. These refer to the Behavioural Inhibition System (BIS), sensitive to negative outcomes and the Behavioural Activation System (BAS), which is sensitive to positive outcomes. The seven BIS items reflect concerns about the possibility of a negative situation, and the five BAS items reflect one's responsiveness to rewards, measured by excitement tendencies or arousal related to positive experiences.

The third measure is the Selves Questionnaire, which assesses the degree of congruency between participants' actual, ideal and ought selves. Promotion and prevention foci are represented by the degree of similarity between individuals' actual and ideal selves, and their actual and ought selves (Brockner et al. 2002). For this method, participants provide six attributes which they would like to possess (ideals) or think they should possess (oughts) in random order. After this, they were asked to list the extent to which they would like to or should possess the attribute. They then indicate the degree to which they currently possess the aforementioned attribute. The differences between actual and either ideal or ought ratings are calculated for each attribute, and then summed to obtain the promotion and prevention focus measures (Higgins et al. 1997).

The measure developed by Lockwood (2002) is used to study motivation initiated by role models. The eighteen items described include tenets of regulatory focus theory, and consider success and failure in goal pursuit, with nine reflective items for promotion and prevention foci. Like the RFQ, the Lockwood (2002) measure also displays a low correlation between the sub-scales.

Based on research conducted by Haws et al. (2010), the RFQ possesses superior comparative performance. However, it suffers from two limitations, which are, an absence of emotional content in its items, and items that are entirely past-oriented. Thus, a composite scale, the CRFS is proposed. It comprises ten items, each five for promotion and prevention focus. Four items from the RFQ (two promotion, two prevention), two from the BIS/BAS scale (one promotion, one prevention) and four items from Lockwood scale (two promotion, two prevention) are utilised for this scale (Haws et al. 2010).

The CRFS covers key tenets of regulatory focus theory, distinguishing between approach and avoidance within each regulatory focus, includes both cognitive and emotional measures and is comprised of past, present and future-oriented items. Haws et al. (2010) demonstrate that the CRFS possesses reliability, homogeneity and predictive validity. Thus, from a scale representativeness perspective, the CRFS overcomes the limitations from which the RFQ, as well as the other scales, individually suffer (Haws et al. 2010). As such, the CRFS has been selected for assessing chronic regulatory focus in this book.

The CRFS uses a seven-point Likert scale ranging from (1) not at all true of me to (7) very true of me. The first five items of the ten item scale are related to the promotion focus, and the last five relate to the prevention focus. If a participant scores higher in the first five, a promotion focus is assigned, and if a participant scores higher in the last five, a prevention focus is assigned. The following section provides a brief overview of the eye tracking measure used to determine the validity of both hypotheses.

3.2.2 Eye Tracking

As indicated in Sect. 3.1, the eye tracker was used as the measure to collect behavioural data regarding the participants' asset and portfolio allocation choices.

The eye tracker is an objective tool (Duchowski 2007) and thus using the eye tracker and the self-report as measures to test the hypotheses will limit the effects of social desirability bias and common method variance (Podsakoff et al. 2003). This section outlines the use of the eye tracker as a measure.

After the chronic regulatory focus of participants was assessed, participants underwent a distraction scenario (Sect. 4.3.2) to prevent them from determining the hypotheses (Shavit et al. 2010). They were then seated in front of the Tobii T120 Eye Tracker to determine which assets and portfolios they looked at for a proportionately longer time. The asset and portfolio that they looked at for a proportionately longer time is deemed to be the selection. Using proportionate viewing time aids in controlling for individual differences (Shavit et al. 2010).

Eye tracking is a technique that collects behavioural data whereby an individual's eye movements are measured so that the researcher knows where a person is looking at any given time, along with the sequence in which their eyes are shifting from one location to another (Poole and Ball 2005). Eye tracking was first used in reading research over 100-years ago (Rayner et al. 2011), and a multitude of studies across various disciplines have been conducted since. Past research has utilised eye tracking to gain insight into various aspects of consumer behaviour (Janiszewski 1998; Rosbergen et al. 1997), indicating the veracity of eye tracking methods in collecting behavioural data.

Most systems today use a 'corneal-reflection/pupil centre' method (Goldberg and Wichansky 2003), consisting of a standard desktop computer with an infrared camera mounted below the display monitor. The infrared light from an LED embedded in the infrared camera is first directed in the eye to create strong reflections in target eye features to make them easier to track. The light enters the retina and a large amount of it is reflected back, making the pupil appear bright and well-defined. The corneal reflection is generated by the infrared light, appearing as a small glint. Once the software has identified the centre of the pupil and the location of the corneal reflection, the vector between is measured, and the point of interest can be found. Video-based eye trackers have to be fine-tuned to the particularities of each person's eye movements by a 'calibration' process. This process is slightly different depending on the system that is being used, and for the Tobii T120, in this book, a 9-point monitor calibration was done.

Eye tracking technology possesses several limits, and these may affect data that is collected. For example, if one is interested in analysing fixations,[2] the equipment must be optimised for such purposes (Karn et al. 2000). Sampling rate is also important, as a 60 Hz rate may be suitable for usability studies, but not for reading research, for example (Rayner et al. 2011). However, the 120 Hz rate of the eye tracker in this experiment is more than sufficient. Eye trackers are generally somewhat sensitive, and can have difficulty tracking participants who wear hard contact lenses and bifocals, as these will interrupt the normal path of a reflection, and thus care was taken in this book to exclude such participants. Those with

[2]Fixation is the maintaining of the visual gaze on a single location.

unusually large pupils or 'lazy eye' may also be incompatible with the hardware. In addition, once calibration is completed, this process should be repeated at regular intervals to maintain an accurate point-of-regard measurement. However, as participants were only in front of the display screen for less than half an hour, this is unnecessary. To ensure that eye movements are properly attributed to actual cognitive processing, the tasks that participants undergo should be well-defined (Just and Carpenter 1976), and visual distractions such as colourful objects around the screen should be eliminated lest when they alter the eye-movement data (Goldberg and Wichansky 2003). It is recommended that the researcher stays out of sight of the participants, and refrains from speaking to them (Strandvall 2013). Moreover, given that eye tracking results in huge amounts of data, it is essential to perform filtering and analysis automatically, to save time and minimise errors through manual data processing. These principles have been taken into account in this book, resulting in a clear and to-the-point experimental design.

Several qualitative data analysis methods exist within the Tobii Eye tracker software, to display the data collected, such as gaze plots, heat maps, cluster visualisations and bee swarm visualisations. Gaze plots show the sequence and positions of fixations on a static media, with the size of the dots indicating the fixation duration and the numbers in the dots representing the order of the fixations, are used to illustrate the gaze patterns of participants. Heat maps use different colours to show the aggregated number of fixations participants made in certain areas, to analyse how long, where and how many times participants look at predefined areas on the screen. Cluster visualisations are aggregated graphic representations of areas with high concentrations of gaze data points. Bee swarm visualisations are dynamic representations for the fixations of a group of participants on top of a selected video, with the fixation of each participant illustrated with a coloured dot (Strandvall 2013). As these are qualitative analysis methods, they were not used in the book, as results from qualitative eye tracker tests are suitable for describing problems and making improvements, not for describing behaviour (Strandvall 2013).

Quantitative eye tracker tests are more suited for generalisation and comparisons between groups, as in this book. Varieties of quantitative methods are used in eye tracking, such as total scanpath length, mean fixation duration and various area-of-interest[3] (AOI) techniques. An AOI technique was used for this book, to see where and how long participants affix their gaze on the various situations displayed. Of the methods available, number of visits and percentage of participants fixating on an AOI have been deemed the most suitable, as these give the most accurate representation of the areas in the display that individuals find most interesting (Strandvall 2013). The number of fixations on an AOI was not used as this can be influenced by AOI size.

[3]AOI techniques refer to displays wherein an area on the screen has been highlighted beforehand, and all fixations within this area will be recorded by the eye-tracking software.

There still exist limitations with the AOI method. As any point within the target area classifies as a fixation point, saccade[4] points leading into a fixation may be included in the final fixation, resulting in misleadingly long durations for identified fixations. Moreover, long saccades through large AOI regions may be identified as fixations, leading to incorrect data analysis (Salvucci and Goldberg 2000), although this effect may be controlled for by recruiting a large number of participants.

Research has shown that fixations and interests are related, and that eye movements reflect the thought process (Yarbus and Riggs 1967). It is hypothesised that when a participant looks at an object, the former thinks about the object as long as the recorded fixation (Just and Carpenter 1980). Visual attention is slightly ahead of the eye, and when attention moves to a new location, the eyes follow suit (Hoffman 1998). As such, the length of fixations recorded on the system may give an indication of the participants' interest in a given allocation scenario. However, given the nature of covert attention,[5] the resulting fixation patterns may not indicate one's attention, but only where the eye has been viewing (Wright and Ward 2008). It is still not possible to infer specific cognitive processes solely from fixation on a particular object in a display (Holsanova 2006). Thus, the purpose of the eye tracker in this book is not to act as a sole test for allocation choice, but to act as a complementary instrument to the self-report. This is hoped to reduce social desirability bias (Podsakoff et al. 2003) and may give insight into the participants' thought process (Yarbus and Riggs 1967).

As detailed earlier, the Tobii T120 Eye Tracker was utilised for this book. It possesses a 120 Hz data rate, freedom of head movement of 30 × 22 × 30 cm, binocular tracking, maximum of 33 ms latency and 300 ms time to tracking recovery. Participants entered the lab individually, and were seated in front of a computer monitor. The next section outlines the research regarding measures of financial literacy, along with how financial literacy was tested.

3.2.3 Financial Literacy

As the book regards financial decision-making, it is necessary to select individuals who are familiar with basic financial products and concepts, or simply those who are financially literate. Several measures exist to determine ones level of financial literacy,[6] such as the Dutch DNB Household Survey, US Health and Retirement Survey (HRS) (Rooij et al. 2012) and Surveys of Consumers (SoC) (Hilgert et al. 2003).

---

[4]Saccades are quick, simultaneous movements of both eyes in the same direction.

[5]Overt attention is the direction of one's senses toward a certain stimulus. Covert attention is the act of focusing on one of several possible stimuli.

[6]Financial literacy is defined as the ability to make informed judgments and to take effective decisions regarding the use and management of money (Noctor et al. 1992).

The DNB household survey is composed of basic questions which tests concepts such as the time value of money, compound interest and inflation and advanced literacy questions which are primarily about the risk and return of assets. The HRS tests concepts relating to interest rates, inflation and risk diversification, whilst the SoC asks about investment behaviours and specific questions about various assets (Hilgert et al. 2003). Specifically amongst students, business students ranked higher in terms of financial literacy (Beal and Delpachitra 2003; Wagland and Taylor 2009), although there is conflicting evidence which suggests that science students outperform business students in some areas, when a test about personal finance knowledge and education is administered (Cull and Whitton 2011). Demographic wise, young adults, women (Lusardi et al. 2010) and low-income groups (Hilgert et al. 2003) are the least financially literate.

Testing financial literacy is a contentious issue as research states that financial education does not have an effect on American high school students (Mandell 2008), whilst some studies indicate a relationship between financial literacy and favourable financial outcomes (Cole and Shastry 2009; Fox et al. 2005; Lusardi 2003). For an individual to be financially literate, they must demonstrate knowledge and skills required to make choices within the financial markets (Huston 2010).

Given the mixed results concerning financial literacy testing by a questionnaire, the screening of participants beforehand may be more effective. Participants from certain demographics, who possess the requisite levels of financial knowledge for this book, were used, such as University employees (Zhou and Pham 2004), final-year undergraduates and postgraduate students. The financial knowledge required for this experiment is covered in postgraduate financial coursework, and where participants have not undergone such coursework, they have to be currently working in financial institutions, or frequently be exposed to financial theory and practice, such as those who work at the Business faculty of a University.

As a check to reconfirm the participants' level of financial literacy, specific questions from the Surveys of Consumers[7] (University of Michigan 2001), was used. The questions were included in the questionnaire given to participants. These questions reconfirm whether participants have the level of financial literacy required to understand the financial components of the experiment. Participants are deemed to have the required level of financial literacy if they answer at least three of the four questions correctly. Gauging financial literacy can be carried out using a few questions (Lusardi 2008), but it was only conducted after the main portion of the experiment. The mere evaluation of financial products can activate states of promotion or prevention (Zhou and Pham 2004), and thus conducting any of the earlier mentioned financial literacy tests prior to the main portion of the experiment may inadvertently prime participants toward certain regulatory foci, affecting the validity of data collected. Due to the contentious nature of testing for financial literacy

[7]Contained in Appendix.

(Mandell 2008; Willis 2008), the test of financial literacy conducted in this book will only be coded as a control variable for the logit model. Further analysis into this variable will not be conducted, as inaccurate conclusions may be drawn. The section that follows describes the research methodology that was used to conduct this book, along with an outline of the procedure that was conducted.

Chapter 4
Research Methodology

Abstract This chapter starts with defining the research methodology used to conduct the research; experimental design. It is followed by an overview of the ethical considerations involved. The procedure used will then be outlined, with a section on sample selection and allocation scenarios. A brief summary of the statistical methods used concludes the chapter.

4.1 Experimental Design

To determine the validity of the hypotheses, the overarching methodology that has been chosen to conduct the research is experimental design, which is defined as the design of any information-gathering exercise where there is variation, regardless of whether the experimenter has full control or not. Experimental design was used as the methodology in this book, as it provides the overall framework for the various methods that were employed.

The crux of experimental research is the question of whether an observed relationship between an action and outcome is truly causal[1] or a false relationship. Experiments are focused heavily on internal validity,[2] with the aim to rule out alternative explanations of the relationship observed between the independent and dependent variables. To rule out additional variables, experimental designs comprise two key features; control and randomisation. Control means that the researcher controls and manipulates the factors of interest, whilst keeping as many other variables as possible constant. Test conditions are standardised to avoid other factors, co-varying and influencing outcomes. Randomisation is utilised when control cannot be achieved by other means. Randomisation involves assigning test

[1]Causality refers to relationships between variables, wherein a change in a variable necessarily results in a change in another variable (Oppewal 2011).

[2]Internal validity is concerned whether an observed relationship is causal. It is the extent to which alternative explanations for an observed relationship between variables can be ruled out (Oppewal 2011).

N. Kumar, *Chronic Regulatory Focus and Financial Decision-Making*,
SpringerBriefs in Finance, DOI 10.1007/978-981-287-694-2_4

units to different conditions based on chance, elaborated upon in Sect. 4.3.2. Experiments are focused on internal validity, but there is always a trade-off with external validity. This refers to whether the observed relationships can be generalised to other samples of people or situations (Oppewal 2011).

To expand on finance and regulatory focus as a whole, the following were utilised; CRFS, eye tracker, self-report and statistical analysis. The work of Scholer et al. (2010) and Zhou and Pham (2004) guided this book. It is hoped that this work will add to what has previously been done in the amalgam of finance and regulatory focus, as well as pioneer future research in this area. As stated in the hypothesis, the aim of this book is to see if chronic regulatory focus has an influence on asset and portfolio decisions.

4.2 Ethical Considerations

As people are involved in this work, there are ethical considerations involved. Participants were completely anonymous, and unidentifiable in the research conducted. At no point of the experiment were details of the participants taken down, or listed in a database. All participants were assigned a unique ID number that was on the asset and allocation form. Ethical clearance was obtained early in the study, as per required guidelines.

4.3 Procedure

The experiment was composed of three stages. In stage 1, participants were asked to fill up the CRFS to determine their chronic regulatory focus. In stage 2, individuals sat in front of the eye tracker, and viewed the asset, then the portfolio scenarios. A larger proportion of time on a particular asset/portfolio indicated a selection, for the particular scenario. In stage 3, participants were given a self-report on which to indicate their asset and portfolio selections, identical to those on the screen. They then filled up a set of questions to reconfirm their financial literacy. The CRFS, allocation scenarios, self-report and financial literacy questions were in the same questionnaire provided to the participants. The results were analysed using SPSS. Table 4.1 illustrates the procedure of the research.

4.3.1 Sample Selection

A total of 105 participants (staff and students, aged 22–70 years, 60 females and 45 males) were recruited from the Malaysian campus of Monash University where the research was conducted, and participants were placed into a single condition. The

Table 4.1 Procedure flowchart

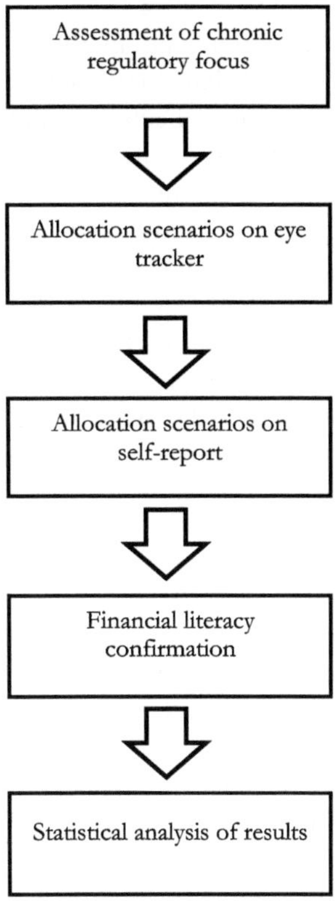

use of college students as subjects for theoretical research is suitable (Calder et al. 1981), especially if strict alpha values are used (Enis et al. 1972). Moreover, the results obtained from student and non-student samples are similar (Beltramini 1983; Sheth 1970). All the students were from the business faculty, about to graduate within few months. They also had worked in various jobs (retail sales associates, private tuition, research assistants, wait staff) for at least ten hours a week and possessed internship experience for few months, as per their course requirements. They were thus deemed to be familiar with the general financial environment and able to relate to financial allocation situations presented. Although the participants did not possess familiarity with the nature of the financial environment similar to that of working adults, they were still suitable candidates for exploratory research on financial decision-making.

Participants were recruited by word-of-mouth, and the experiment was made known to all suitable groups, i.e. staff and third-year students. Each subset of *n* individuals had the same probability of being chosen as another subset of *n* individuals (Yates et al. 2002). Simple random sampling is thus the technique applied. The study was advertised to a diverse group of participants, to minimise the effects of culture affecting the results, as denoted in the following sections.

4.3.1.1 Regulatory Focus and Culture

The demographic profile of the participants involved was typical of a university in Malaysia with a higher number of Asians than other ethnic groups. As the majority of participants were of Asian descent (collectivist cultures), this may predicate them to be of a particular chronic regulatory focus. The promotion system is more chronically accessible for people from individualist cultures, and the prevention system is more accessible for people from collectivist cultures (Lee et al. 2000).

However, it is proposed that students in a cosmopolitan and highly ranked university, would be exposed to a wide variety of ideas and modes of thought that may run contrary to their existing biases and regulatory foci. As such, it is predicted that an even split of chronic promotion and prevention participants would be observed, instead of most participants being chronic prevention focused, as predicated by their collectivist background.

4.3.1.2 Culture and Risk-Seeking

As this book concerns financial decision-making, the effect of the participants' culture on their risk attitudes is of concern. As indicated, most of the participants are from collectivist cultural backgrounds. Those from a collectivist society are more risk-seeking than those from individualist societies, perhaps those from collectivist societies are more likely to receive financial help if they are in need (Hsee and Weber 1999; Mandel 2003; Weber and Hsee 1998, 2000).

For studies conducted in the cosmopolitan environment of a highly ranked university, participants would be exposed to various modes of thought, both individualist and collectivist. This would minimise the effects of the inherent risk preferences. As long as financial literacy is controlled , other factors are unlikely to affect the results of the experiment, despite it being conducted in an Asian-based University. The next section looks into the asset and portfolio selections that will be measured by the eye tracker and self-report.

4.3.2 Allocation Scenarios

Participants will be shown the allocation scenarios twice in the experiment. First on the eye tracker, and then on the self-report. As indicated, the hypotheses will be assessed by two instruments (eye tracker, self-report). On the eye tracker, participants indicated their selection/preference by looking at an asset or portfolio for a proportionately longer amount of time. Participants indicated their selection on the self-report with a tick in the box, as in Tables 4.2 and 4.3. Table 4.2 represents the asset allocation scenario and Table 4.3 represents the portfolio allocation scenario. The left boxes in the allocation diagrams represent the promotion scenarios and the right diagrams represent prevention situations. The situations were not labelled to prevent association with promotion and prevention, and appeared in random order, with some participants seeing the promotion and prevention situations on the left and right respectively, and for some the order was reversed. This is to ensure that the orientations of the allocation scenarios do not affect the results.

To prevent participants from inferring the hypotheses of the experiment, they were asked to write a short essay about how their day went.[3] The question was kept as brief as possible, to ensure that it does not influence the allocation scenario that follows. In a previous study, participants were asked to look at visual illusions instead (Shavit et al. 2010). However, this may not be sufficiently distracting, and the essays written may provide further insight into one's regulatory foci.

In previous research (Zhou and Pham 2004), participants were allowed to distribute the funds they received between the assets as they wished, by indicating how much they would like to allocate into each asset, and how much they prefer each asset, on a scale. However, in this experiment, a scale for participants to indicate their preferences was not provided. Displaying a scale on the eye tracker would result in too many AOIs, which would impair the identification of the most preferred situation on the eye tracker. The eye tracker is a measure for the association between chronic regulatory focus and the allocation scenarios, and thus it is imperative that the results from this measure are unbiased. With multiple AOIs, spurious results may occur, as participants would have far too many areas on the screen to focus on. To overcome this issue, the allocation situations are phrased such that participants would indicate where they would like to place *more* of the funds they receive.

An AOI was drawn around each of the assets and portfolios. The time participants spend looking at the various AOIs was measured, with the time spent blinking or observing elements that are irrelevant, such as looking at the keyboard or mouse, excluded. The proportion of time spent by a particular participant on the AOI, indicated the selection. For example, if a person spends proportionately more time on the promotion AOI than compared to the prevention AOI, a promotion selection is assumed.

Stocks are associated with promotion, and mutual funds are identified with prevention (Zhou and Pham 2004). It is not yet known whether chronic regulatory focus affects portfolio allocation, and it is hypothesised that promotion-focused individuals prefer portfolios that may increase, but possibly also decrease in value over time, and prevention-focused individuals prefer those which maintain their value over time, accounting for inflation. This is based on concepts drawn from existing research (Roese et al. 1999; Scholer et al. 2010; Zhou and Pham 2004).

In the allocation scenarios, the means by which the funds are obtained are left unspecified. This phrasing is based on research conducted by Zhou and Pham (2004). The most neutral phrasing for the allocation scenarios is preferred, lest the means by which the funds are obtained affects how the participants allocate the latter. In the scenarios, $6000 is the amount participants have been allocated. This

[3]Contained in Appendix.

Table 4.2 Asset allocation situation

<table>
<tr><td colspan="2">Imagine you have $6000 available and can allocate it in either one of the two groups of assets, as below.

In which group would you put more of your funds?

Indicate your selection, via a tick in the box below.</td></tr>
<tr><td>Stocks</td><td>Mutual Funds</td></tr>
<tr><td></td><td></td></tr>
</table>

Table 4.3 Portfolio allocation situation

<table>
<tr><td colspan="2">Imagine you have $6000 available and can allocate it in either one of the two portfolios, as below.

In which group would you put more of your funds?

Both portfolios account for inflation

Indicate your selection, via a tick in the box below.</td></tr>
<tr><td>Option A</td><td>Option B</td></tr>
<tr><td>High gains, and possible losses, may not maintain value over time</td><td>No gains, and no losses, will maintain value over time</td></tr>
<tr><td></td><td></td></tr>
</table>

may be of different value to participants from varying backgrounds, as $6000 may be important to someone earning $10,000 a year, but irrelevant to someone earning $200,000 a year. To mitigate such effects, a wide variety of participants were drawn upon. Moreover, in the study conducted by Zhou and Pham (2004), a value of $2000 was assigned for the asset allocation scenarios, with no unusual results.

Zhou and Pham (2004) also used an inheritance scenario, that did not appear to bias the decisions of participants. This is possibly due to limited information given about the source of money, apart from it being 'inherited', and that the primary scope of the text was the allocation situations, rather than the source of funds. However, there exists conflicting research on how inherited funds are treated. It is known that wealth that results from windfalls is rarely saved (Imbens et al. 2001; Zagorsky 2013) and that inheritance tends to increase the possibility of retirement (Brown et al. 2010). On the other hand, studies also state that keeping or investing money appears to be the most common outcome with regard to inheritances (Finch and Mason 2000), perhaps because inherited money is viewed to be 'special' and should be treated differently from other money (Rowlingson and McKay 2005). Given the mixed findings regarding inherited funds and to minimise any bias in how participants allocated the funds received, a very brief and neutral scenario (non-inheritance) was used.

4.3.2.1 Selection of Assets and Portfolios

Asset and portfolio allocation scenarios have been used instead of the asset and account allocation scenarios in previous research (Zhou and Pham 2004). Asset allocation is representative of some of the investment decisions that consumers tend to make, and the assets selected are known to be sensitive to different regulatory systems (Zhou and Pham 2004). Portfolio allocation, is more directly reflective of the regulatory focus concept of 'promotion being interested in gaining additions, and prevention concerned with preventing subtractions' (Roese et al. 1999), than when compared to account allocation scenarios in previous research (Zhou and Pham 2004). Portfolios represent a greater portion of the financial allocation decisions undertaken by consumers, as indicated in Sect. 3.1. Portfolio allocation thus acts as a complement to the asset allocation scenarios, to reflect more of the financial choices consumers make.

The relationship between portfolio allocation scenarios and one's chronic regulatory focus has not been empirically tested. Thus, measures were undertaken to make sure that they would yield accurate results. A semi-structured interview was conducted, with a chronic promotion-focused person, who selected both the promotion assets and portfolios. The portfolio allocation scenarios were then reviewed by academics familiar with the relevant theories. A pilot study was also conducted, in which 15 participants were asked to write briefly about what they felt with regard to the portfolio allocation scenarios. Participants indicated that both scenarios should provide the same amount of information and be about the same length. The portfolio allocation scenarios were then made more concise. Participants stated that this made the scenarios easier to comprehend. The following section outlines the statistical methods used to analyse the data collected from the eye tracker and self-report.

4.3.3 Statistical Analysis

For this book, the data collected is in terms of categorical variables, such as the participants' regulatory focus and eye tracker selection.[4] The relationship between categorical variables can be explored with cross tabulation, and the Pearson chi-squared test was applied. The chi-squared test investigates whether there exists a significant association between two categorical variables, but does not indicate the strength of association (Field 2009). To gain insight into the strength and direction of effect for the particular variables, and to control for other variables, a simple logit model is suitable. The participants' asset and portfolio selections (eye tracker, self-report) were used as the dependent variables, in each individual logit model. The validity of the hypotheses was be explored, followed by further analyses. The process and relevant results will be explained in the following chapters.

[4]If promotion-focused participants spent proportionately more time on the promotion assets or portfolios, it will lead to the conclusion that they have selected promotion-based assets or portfolios, with the same going for prevention-focused participants.

Chapter 5
Results

Abstract This chapter first outlines the demographic profile for the participants and the descriptives for chronic regulatory focus, financial literacy, eye tracker—asset selection, eye tracker—portfolio selection, self-report—asset selection and self-report—portfolio selection. Tests of the hypotheses then follow, first with the eye tracker as the measure then followed by the self-report. The chapter is concluded with a section on the further analysis conducted. The further analysis primarily regards the gender and education variables, along with analysis into the effect of the unfavourable world financial outlook.

5.1 Descriptives

This section details with the demographic profile of the participants in the experiment, followed by the descriptives of the variables (chronic regulatory focus, financial literacy, eye tracker—asset selection, eye tracker—portfolio selection, self-report—asset selection and self-report—portfolio selection) that were assessed by a measure (CRFS, financial literacy questionnaire, eye tracker, self-report).

5.1.1 Demographic Profile

The data was collected at a university located in Selangor, Malaysia. A total of 105 participants were involved in the experiment, 60 were females and 45 were males. The Australian participants (two in total) indicated that they were not familiar with the term 'mutual funds', and further ten participants who reported identical scores for the promotion and prevention items in the CRFS were excluded. A chronic regulatory focus cannot be determined for participants who have the same promotion and prevention scores in the CRFS (ten in total). This made an effective

N. Kumar, *Chronic Regulatory Focus and Financial Decision-Making*,
SpringerBriefs in Finance, DOI 10.1007/978-981-287-694-2_5

Table 5.1 Demographic profile

Gender	Female	52
	Male	41
Age group	<30	53
	>30	40
Ethnicity	Caucasian	5
	Non-caucasian	87
Marital status	Married	29
	Single	64
Education	Basic degree	54
	Higher degree	39

sample of 93 participants. The demographic profile of the final sample used in the analysis is noted in Table 5.1.

For 'marital status', participants who indicated 'partnered' and 'attached' were subsumed under 'married'. Regarding 'education', those indicating 'masters' and 'PhD' were grouped under 'higher degree'.

The demographic profile of the participants reflected the typical profile of a university in Malaysia with a higher number of Asians than other ethnic groups, all participants had degrees, with a greater number of participants holding basic degrees. Those who had higher degrees were academics employed at the university. There was also slightly more participants who were under 30-years old. A slightly higher number of females than males participated in the experiment. The participants were either students, academics or professional administrative staff.

5.1.2 Descriptives of Measured Variables

This section outlines the descriptives of the following variables; chronic regulatory focus, financial literacy, eye tracker—asset selection, eye tracker—portfolio selection, self-report—asset selection and self-report—portfolio selection (see Table 5.2).

Participants with the same promotion and prevention scores were excluded, as within the constraints of this research, they cannot be assigned a chronic regulatory focus. Initially, only participants who had a difference of three between their promotion and prevention scores were included in the book. However, reducing this threshold to two, then to one, yielded no significant change in results. Thus, the participants who had promotion and prevention scores with a difference of one and greater were included.

Table 5.2 states that there were slightly more chronic promotion-focused participants than chronic prevention-focused participants. Most participants passed the

Table 5.2 Descriptives of measured variables

Chronic regulatory focus	Promotion	50
	Prevention	43
Financial literacy	Y	65
	N	28
Eye tracker—asset selection	Promotion	24
	Prevention	69
Eye tracker—portfolio selection	Promotion	32
	Prevention	61
Self-report—asset selection	Promotion	40
	Prevention	53
Self-report—portfolio selection	Promotion	50
	Prevention	43

financial literacy questionnaire, correctly answering three out of four questions correctly. On the eye tracker, most participants selected the prevention asset and portfolio. On the self-report, most participants selected the prevention asset, but were slightly more likely to select the promotion portfolio.

5.2 Validity of Hypotheses

Tests of the hypotheses were explored in this section. The main hypotheses will be explored, followed by the additional hypotheses. As indicated, two instruments (eye tracker and self-report) were used to validate the hypotheses. The eye tracker was first used to assess the validity of the hypotheses. The self-report was then applied to test the hypotheses. This section will first report the eye tracker results followed by the results from the self-report, for each individual hypothesis. For the eye tracker, the participant indicated a selection by looking at a particular asset or portfolio for a proportionately longer time. For the self-report, the asset and portfolio selection is indicated by the participant on the paper provided. SPSS was used to conduct the tests of association and the logistic regression. Tests of association were done via the Pearson chi-squared test and Fisher's exact test. For the chi-squared test, asymptotic significance is used (Mehta et al. 1984). For samples that are too small for chi-squared analysis, Fisher's exact test is utilised (Upton 1992). A significance level of $p = 0.05$ (one sided) is assumed for the chi-squared and Fisher's exact test. Given the small number of participants, the statistical power of the analysis is limited and a single tailed significance level of $p = 0.10$ (one sided) is assumed for the logit model (Egger et al. 1997; Sterne et al. 2000). As indicated in Sect. 5.1, there was an effective sample of 93 participants. For the logistic regression, the variables were coded as per Table 5.3.

Table 5.3 Logit model variable coding

Variable	0	1
Age	<30	>30
Education	Basic degree	Higher degree
Ethnicity	Asian	Non-Asian
Gender	M	F
Marital status	Single	Married
Eye tracker—asset selection	Promotion	Prevention
Eye tracker—portfolio selection	Promotion	Prevention
Regulatory focus	Promotion	Prevention
Self-report—asset selection	Promotion	Prevention
Self-report—portfolio selection	Promotion	Prevention
Financial literacy	Y	N

5.2.1 Validity of H1: Eye Tracker

H1 tests the association between chronic regulatory focus and asset allocation. To test this association, an eye tracker was used, followed by a self-report. This section determines the relationship between chronic regulatory focus and asset allocation, with the eye tracker as a measure. The chi-squared test was first conducted to test this association. Table 5.4 indicates the chi-squared result for the association between regulatory focus and asset allocation for the eye tracker. There is a main effect of eye tracker—asset on regulatory focus, ($n = 93$, $\chi^2 = 3.442$, $p < 0.05$). However, as in Table 5.4, participants do not choose the assets that are associated with their regulatory foci. H1 is unsupported by the chi-squared test, with the eye tracker as the measure.

To gain further insight into the relationship between chronic regulatory focus and the asset selections on the eye tracker, a logistic regression was conducted. The logistic regression controlled for the effect of other variables is to indicate the strength and direction of the relationship between chronic regulatory focus and asset selections on the eye tracker.

Table 5.4 Basic Pearson chi-squared test and cross tabulation for regulatory focus * eye tracker—asset allocation

		Value	df	Asymp. sig. (1-sided)	
Pearson chi-square		3.442	1	0.032	
		Eye tracker—asset			Total
		Promotion		Prevention	
Regulatory focus	Promotion	9		41	50
	Prevention	15		28	43
Total		24		69	93

Table 5.5 Logit model for eye tracker—asset selection against age, education, ethnicity, marital status, regulatory focus, financial literacy, gender

Dependent variable	−2 Log likelihood	Cox and Snell R square	Nagelkerke R square
Eye tracker—asset selection	96.998	0.114	0.166
Variable	β	S.E.	Sig.
Age	−0.297	0.918	0.373
Education	−0.660	1.003	0.256
Ethnicity	0.937	1.202	0.218
Gender	1.027	0.542	0.029
Marital status	0.812	0.764	0.144
Regulatory focus	−1.166	0.532	0.014
Financial literacy	−0.899	0.539	0.048
Constant	1.491	0.58	0.005

Eye tracker—asset selection was the dependent variable, and age, education, ethnicity, marital status, regulatory focus, financial literacy and gender are the independent variables for the logit model performed and this is indicated in Table 5.5.

Regulatory focus ($\beta = -1.166, p < 0.10$), financial literacy ($\beta = -0.899, p < 0.10$) and gender (β = 1.027, p < 0.10) are significant. Although regulatory focus is significant, the results indicate that prevention-focused participants are less likely to look at the prevention assets, and promotion-focused participants are less likely to look at promotion assets (see Sect. 6.1.2). This is in opposition to H1. Thus, using the eye tracker as a measure, H1 is unsupported by the logit model.

Participants with a low financial literacy score are less likely to look at the prevention asset for a proportionately longer time, than compared to those with a high financial literacy score. Female participants are more likely to look at the prevention asset for a proportionately longer time, compared to male participants. Although H1 is unsupported by the eye tracker measure, significant results are obtained for financial literacy and gender. Further analysis will be conducted in later sections, to gain more insight. The next section will determine the validity of H1 with the self-report as the measure.

5.2.2 *Validity of H1: Self-report*

A self-report was used after the eye tracker to determine the validity of H1. This section regards the results obtained using the self-report. The chi-squared test was first conducted to determine association between regulatory focus and asset allocation on the self-report. The cross tabulation is denoted in Table 5.6. Significant results were not reported (n = 93, χ^2 = 0.43, p > 0.05) for the chi-squared test, and

Table 5.6 Cross tabulation for regulatory focus * self-report—asset allocation

		Self-report—asset		Total
		Promotion	Prevention	
Regulatory focus	Promotion	22	28	50
	Prevention	18	25	43
Total		40	53	93

for the association between regulatory focus and self-report—asset allocation. H1 is unsupported by the chi-squared analysis, and for the self-report.

Although the chi-squared results are insignificant, further insight may be gained by controlling for other variables, and a logit regression was thus conducted. In Table 5.7, self-report—asset selection is the dependent variable, and age, education, ethnicity, marital status, regulatory focus, financial literacy and gender are the independent variables. Table 5.7 indicates no significant results for the logit model. H1 is not supported by the logistic regression, with the self-report as the measure.

Overall, H1 is unsupported, regardless of the measure used. Participants do not appear to choose assets that are associated with their chronic regulatory foci. It is postulated that the negative world financial outlook may be influencing the majority of participants to select the prevention asset on both measures. This effect will be explored in later sections. The following section will determine the validity of H2, with the eye tracker and self-report as the measure.

5.2.3 *Validity of H2: Eye Tracker*

H2 tests the association between chronic regulatory focus and portfolio allocations, first with the eye tracker, followed by the self-report. This section determines the

Table 5.7 Logit model for self-report—asset selection against age, education, ethnicity, gender, marital status, regulatory focus, financial literacy

Dependent variable	−2 Log likelihood	Cox and Snell R square	Nagelkerke R square
Self-report—asset selection	120.380	0.042	0.056
Variable	β	S.E.	Sig.
Age	−0.344	0.793	0.488
Education	0.852	0.845	0.157
Ethnicity	−0.093	0.998	0.463
Gender	0.298	0.464	0.260
Marital status	0.171	0.675	0.400
Regulatory focus	0.116	0.450	0.399
Financial literacy	0.633	0.494	0.100
Constant	−0.373	0.488	0.222

Table 5.8 Cross tabulation for regulatory focus * eye tracker—portfolio allocation

		Eye tracker—portfolio		Total
		Promotion	Prevention	
Regulatory focus	Promotion	18	32	50
	Prevention	14	29	43
Total		32	61	93

association between chronic regulatory focus and portfolio allocation, with the eye tracker as a measure. A chi-squared test was first conducted to test this association. Table 5.8 indicates the cross tabulation between regulatory focus and eye tracker—portfolio. No significant results were reported ($n = 93$, $\chi^2 = 0.121$, $p > 0.05$). The chi-squared analysis does not support H2, with the eye tracker as the measure.

Although the chi-squared results are insignificant, greater insight may be gained by controlling other variables, and thus a logit regression was conducted. Table 5.9 indicates that eye tracker—portfolio selection is the dependent variable, and age, education, ethnicity, marital status, regulatory focus, financial literacy and gender are the independent variables in the regression. Table 5.9 states that there are no significant results for regulatory focus in the logit model. H2 is thus unsupported by the logistic regression, with the eye tracker as the measure.

Although Table 5.9 states that H2 is unsupported by the eye tracker, financial literacy is significant ($\beta = -1.014$, $p < 0.10$). This means that those who have a low financial literacy score are less likely to look at the prevention portfolio for a proportionately longer time. The next section will determine the validity of H2 with the self-report as the measure.

Table 5.9 Logit model for eye tracker—portfolio selection against age, education, ethnicity, gender, marital status, regulatory focus, financial literacy

Dependent variable	−2 Log likelihood	Cox and Snell R square	Nagelkerke R square
Eye tracker—portfolio selection	110.899	0.077	0.108
Variable	β	S.E.	Sig.
Age	−0.953	0.900	0.145
Education	0.549	0.952	0.282
Ethnicity	−0.742	0.960	0.220
Gender	0.601	0.489	0.110
Marital status	0.758	0.737	0.152
Regulatory focus	0.128	0.472	0.394
Financial literacy	−1.014	0.500	0.021
Constant	0.627	0.515	0.112

5.2.4 *Validity of H2: Self-report*

The measure of interest for this section was the portfolio selection indicated on the self-report, instead of the eye tracker in the previous section. A chi-squared test was first conducted to determine association between regulatory focus and portfolio allocation (H2). The cross tabulation is denoted in Table 5.10. No significant results were reported ($n = 93$, $\chi^2 = 0.218$, $p > 0.05$). The chi-squared test does not support H2, with the self-report as the measure.

Although the chi-squared results are insignificant, further understanding may be obtained by controlling for other variables, and a logit regression was performed. Table 5.11, as below, indicates that self-report—portfolio selection is the dependent variable, and age, education, ethnicity, marital status, regulatory focus, financial literacy and gender are the independent variables. Table 5.11 indicates that there are no significant results for regulatory focus in the logit model. H2 is not supported by the logistic regression, when the self-report is utilised as the measure.

Although H2 is unsupported by the self-report, Table 5.11 indicates that gender is significant ($\beta = -0.663$, $p < 0.10$). This indicates that females are less likely than males to select a prevention rather than promotion portfolio. Further analysis on gender will be conducted in later sections, to gain additional insight.

Table 5.10 Cross tabulation for regulatory focus * portfolio allocation (self-report)

		Self-report—portfolio		Total
		Promotion	Prevention	
Regulatory focus	Promotion	28	22	50
	Prevention	22	21	43
Total		50	43	93

Table 5.11 Logit model for self-report—portfolio selection against age, education, ethnicity, gender, marital status, regulatory focus, financial literacy

Dependent variable	−2 Log likelihood	Cox and Snell R square	Nagelkerke R square
Self-report—portfolio selection	122.082	0.068	0.091
Variable	β	S.E.	Sig.
Age	0.409	0.807	0.306
Education	−0.707	0.854	0.204
Ethnicity	−0.382	0.977	0.348
Gender	−0.663	0.471	0.080
Marital status	−0.764	0.674	0.129
Regulatory focus	0.177	0.444	0.345
Financial literacy	0.222	0.48	0.322
Constant	0.506	0.494	0.153

On the eye tracker, most participants selected the prevention portfolio, but were almost equally likely to select either portfolio or the self-report. Overall, H2 is unsupported by the data, regardless of the measure used. This is purported to be due to the effect of the adverse world financial outlook, causing participants to select portfolios that are not in accordance with their chronic regulatory focus.

5.2.5 Validity of Main Hypotheses: Summary

Both H1 and H2 are unsupported by the data, regardless of the measure used; eye tracker or self-report. The effect of the negative world financial climate is purported to have influenced participants by selecting the assets and portfolios that are not in accordance with their chronic regulatory foci. This effect will be elaborated upon in section.

5.2.6 Financial Outlook

In Sect. 5.2, both hypotheses were unsupported, regardless of the measure used. It is proposed that the effect of the harsh world financial outlook influenced the participants to select the assets and portfolios that were not in accordance with their regulatory focus. In the pilot study, preliminary statistics indicated that participants were not selecting assets and portfolios according to their chronic regulatory focus, i.e. promotion-focused participants were not selecting promotion assets and portfolios, and prevention-focused participants were not selecting prevention assets and portfolios. To determine the effect of the unfavourable world financial climate, the latter half of the participants (58) were asked to write their answer to the following open-ended question:

> What do you feel about the global financial situation?

The above question was placed in the questionnaire after completion of the test for financial literacy. The responses to this question were then coded, with magnitude coding (Saldaña 2012) into the following categories 'Positive', 'Negative' and 'Indifferent'. Examples of these responses and their corresponding codes are as follows.

5.2.6.1 Positive

> It's definitely fluctuating but I think these things will eventually balance out as they usually do.

> I'm not an economist so I don't know what the real situation is. However, I feel that there isn't a major crisis (not more so than in previous occasions). In fact, I feel that on the contrary there appears to be economic growth and development in Asia.

The 'Positive' code was assigned when participants', as above, indicated that they felt the world financial outlook was positive, or improving.

5.2.6.2 Negative

> I feel that the current global financial situation is getting worse. Further, it will worsen due to Europe's crisis and the Middle East Crisis as well.

> Beyond Rubbish!! I came to this conclusion based on the following factors. The capitalist economic system is based on resource savvy, power hungry principles which would make a few people (<1% global population) rich. These individuals/countries/corporation tends (sic) to make economic bubbles for their betterment, which would shoot 95% of the world population into economic stride. I do not believe in finances such as in currency and only believe in resources, such as oil, gold, etc. I feel the current global financial situation would deteriorate even further and collapse taking the entire world with it.

The 'Negative' code was assigned when the participant indicated that the world financial outlook was worsening, or in a poor state.

5.2.6.3 Indifferent

> I'm oblivious to the global financial situation. However, it should be rather okay I suppose based on the fact that I'm nowhere close to eating grass.

> To be honest quite indifferent as someone else handles my portfolio. Terrible but true.

'Indifferent' was assigned when the participant indicated that they did not care or unaware of the global financial outlook.

5.2.6.4 Descriptives

After coding was completed, most of the participants were assigned a 'Negative' world outlook, as indicated in Table 5.11a. Fifty eight participants answered the open-ended question, as it was provided for only the latter half of the participants.

Financial outlook was postulated to influence participants to select the asset and portfolio that were not associated with their chronic regulatory focus. The significant results in Sect. 5.3.3 indicate that asset and portfolio selections on the self-report

Table 5.11a Breakdown of financial outlook

Financial Outlook	Positive	11
	Negative	41
	Indifferent	6

Table 5.11b Fisher's exact test and cross tabulation for Regulatory focus * asset allocation (positive outlook)

	Value	df	Asymp. Sig. (1-sided)
Pearson Chi-Square	5.238	1	0.011

		Self-report—asset		Total
		Promotion	Prevention	
Regulatory focus	Promotion	4	2	6
	Prevention	0	5	5
Total		4	7	11

were associated. Financial outlook is also proposed to be related to asset and portfolio allocation decisions. Thus, examining participants by their financial outlook, and then testing the association between regulatory focus and asset/portfolio allocation, further insight may be gleaned. The next section outlines the findings.

5.2.6.5 Regulatory Focus * Asset and Portfolio Selection: Financial Outlook

As financial outlook is purported to affect asset and portfolio selection, segmenting the participants by their financial outlook and then testing for association between regulatory focus and the selections made may yield further insights. Significant results were only obtained for the association between regulatory focus and self-report—asset selection, for those with a positive outlook, as indicated in Table 5.11b. No significant results were obtained for the association between regulatory focus and self-report—portfolio selection, eye tracker—asset selection and eye tracker—portfolio selection.

Table 5.11b indicates a main effect of regulatory focus on self-report—asset selection ($n = 11$, Fisher's exact test = 0.045, $p < 0.05$) for the positive group. Fisher's exact test is used as the expected count as less than 5 (Upton 1992), thus making this test of association unsuitable for the Pearson chi-squared test (Mehta et al. 1984). Table 5.11b states that participants with a chronic promotion focus were fairly evenly distributed across the promotion and prevention allocation scenarios, i.e. they had an equal chance of choosing a prevention or promotion asset. However, all participants with a chronic prevention focus selected the prevention asset, instead of the promotion asset. The next section details analysis into the further hypotheses.

5.3 Further Hypotheses

This section will explore the additional hypotheses, concerning gender, education and age. Only significant results are stated.

5.3.1 *Validity of Ha*

Research indicates that gender is associated with risk preferences, with female investors exhibiting more risk aversion than male investors (Barsky et al. 1997). Regulatory focus is known to be associated with risk preferences as well (Kirmani and Zhu 2007). Gender and regulatory focus may thus affect risk preferences in tandem. In this book, risk preferences are modelled by financial allocation decisions.

To explore the hypothesis, participants were divided into groups based on their gender. A chi-squared analysis was then conducted to determine the association between the selections made and the regulatory focus. Significant results were only obtained for females in association between regulatory focus and eye tracker—asset selection, regulatory focus and self-report—asset selection, regulatory focus and self-report—portfolio selection. Significant results were not obtained for the association between regulatory focus and eye tracker—portfolio selections. The relationship between gender and regulatory focus on the eye tracker selections will first be explored, followed by the selections on the self-report.

5.3.1.1 Validity of Hα: Eye Tracker

This section explores Hα, the relationship between regulatory focus, eye tracker—asset selections and gender. As indicated, significant results were not observed for the relationship between regulatory focus, eye tracker—portfolio selections and gender. Table 5.12 indicates that when only female participants are included, a chi-square test for the association between regulatory focus and eye tracker—asset selection, yields a main effect, but at the $p = 0.10$ level ($n = 52$, $\chi^2 = 1.853$, $p < 0.10$). Table 5.12 states that 88 % of the females with a chronic promotion focus selected the promotion asset on the eye tracker. 70.4 % of females with a chronic prevention focus selected the prevention asset.

To gain further understanding into the relationship between gender, regulatory focus and the eye tracker selections, a logit model was made to run with eye tracker—asset selection is the dependent variable; age, education, ethnicity, marital status, regulatory focus, financial literacy and gender as the independent variables. The logit model with eye tracker—asset selection as the dependent variable is on the following page, Table 5.13.

Table 5.12 Basic Pearson chi-squared test and cross tabulation for regulatory focus * eye tracker—asset allocation (female)

	Value	df	Asymp. sig. (1-sided)
Pearson chi-square	2.419	1	0.060

		Eye tracker—asset		Total
		Promotion	Prevention	
Regulatory focus	Promotion	3	22	25
	Prevention	8	19	27
Total		11	41	52

Table 5.13 Logit model for eye tracker—asset selection against age, education, ethnicity, marital status, regulatory focus, financial literacy, gender

Dependent variable	−2 Log likelihood	Cox and Snell R square	Nagelkerke R square
Eye tracker—asset selection	96.998	0.114	0.166
Variable	β	S.E.	Sig.
Age	−0.297	0.918	0.373
Education	−0.660	1.003	0.256
Ethnicity	0.937	1.202	0.218
Gender	1.027	0.542	0.029
Marital status	0.812	0.764	0.144
Regulatory focus	−1.166	0.532	0.014
Financial literacy	−0.899	0.539	0.048
Constant	1.491	0.58	0.005

Gender ($\beta = 1.027$, $p < 0.10$) is significant. This indicates that females are more likely to look at prevention assets than males. An interaction term, regulatory focus*gender was then added to gain further insight into the relationship between regulatory focus and gender, but did not yield significant results.

A logistic regression was then performed with eye tracker—portfolio selection as the dependent variable and age, education, ethnicity, marital status, regulatory focus, financial literacy and gender as the independent variables. However, as indicated in Sect. 5.2.3 no significant results were obtained for gender. An interaction term was then added, regulatory focus * gender, comprised of the regulatory focus and gender variables. This was to gain greater understanding of the relationship between regulatory focus and gender. No significant results were observed. The following section will explore the relationship between the selections on the self-report and gender.

5.3.1.2 Validity of Hα: Self-report

This section explores the relationship between chronic regulatory focus, the self-report selections (asset, portfolio) and gender. A chi-squared analysis was first conducted for the association between regulatory focus and asset selections on the self-report, for both genders. Table 5.14 indicates that when only female participants are included, a chi-squared test for the association between regulatory focus and self-report—asset selection, yielded a main effect, but at the $p = 0.10$ level ($n = 52$, $\chi^2 = 1.853$, $p < 0.10$). Table 5.14 also states that 66.7 % of the females with a chronic prevention focus selected the prevention asset. No significant results were obtained for males.

To gain greater understanding into the effect of regulatory focus and gender on asset allocation (self-report), a logit regression was performed. Self-report—asset selection was the dependent variable, and age, education, ethnicity, marital status,

Table 5.14 Basic Pearson chi-squared test and cross tabulation for regulatory focus * self-report—asset (female)

		Value	df	Asymp. sig. (1-sided)	
Pearson chi-aquare		1.853	1	0.089	
		Self-report—asset			Total
		Promotion		Prevention	
Regulatory focus	Promotion	13		12	25
	Prevention	9		18	27
Total		22		30	52

regulatory focus, financial literacy, gender and regulatory focus * gender were elicited as independent variables. No significant results were observed. The following section focuses on the relationship between portfolio selection on the self-report, regulatory focus and gender.

A chi-squared test of association was then performed to test the relationship between the portfolio selections on the self-report, and regulatory focus, examining participants based on their gender. No significant results were observed for males. Table 5.15 indicates the cross tabulations and chi-squared results regarding regulatory focus and self-report—portfolio selection, for females.

Table 5.15 indicates that when only female participants are included, a chi-squared test for the association between regulatory focus and self-report—portfolio selection, yields a main effect ($n = 52$, $\chi^2 = 2.920$, $p < 0.05$). Table 5.15 states that 68 % of the females with a chronic promotion focus select the promotion portfolio. No significant results were obtained for males.

To gain greater insight into the effects of regulatory focus and gender on portfolio selection on the self-report, a logistic regression was performed with self-report—portfolio selection as the dependent variable, and age, education, ethnicity, marital status, regulatory focus, financial literacy, gender and regulatory focus * gender as independent variables. The interaction term, regulatory focus * gender, comprised of the regulatory focus and gender variables was added to obtain further understanding into the effect of gender and regulatory focus on portfolio allocation. Table 5.16, indicates the results in the following page.

As in Table 5.16a, the interaction term, regulatory focus * gender was significant ($\beta = 1.736$, $p < 0.10$) as was gender ($\beta = -1.480$, $p < 0.10$). Females are less likely to select a prevention portfolio. However, the relationship is weaker for females

Table 5.15 Basic pearson chi-squared test and cross tabulation for Regulatory focus * self-report—portfolio (female)

		Value	df	Asymp. sig. (1-sided)	
Pearson chi-square		2.920	1	0.044	
		Self-report—asset			Total
		Promotion		Prevention	
Regulatory focus	Promotion	17		8	25
	Prevention	12		15	27
Total		29		23	52

Table 5.16 Logit model for self-report—portfolio selection against age, education, ethnicity, marital status, regulatory focus, financial literacy, gender, regulatory focus * gender

Dependent variable	−2 Log likelihood	Cox and Snell R square	Nagelkerke R square
Self-report—portfolio selection	118.407	0.104	0.139
Variable	*β*	S.E.	Sig.
Age	0.464	0.819	0.286
Education	−0.688	0.868	0.214
Ethnicity	−0.34	1.015	0.369
Marital status	−0.873	0.691	0.103
Regulatory focus	−0.792	0.684	0.124
Financial literacy	0.054	0.500	0.457
Gender	−1.480	0.653	0.012
Regulatory focus * gender	1.736	0.918	0.030
Constant	0.956	0.564	0.045

Table 5.16a Age groups of participants

Age group	No. of participants
20–30	59
31–40	16
41–50	21
51–60	9

with a chronic prevention focus. This result may indicate the relative strength of the prevention focus over the promotion focus.

The results state that females more likely look at prevention assets than males. Also, females are less likely to select the prevention portfolio on the self-report, but this effect is weaker for females who are chronic prevention-focused. The following section states the analysis into Hβ.

5.3.2 *Validity of Hβ*

Insight into Hβ was obtained by dividing participants based on their age (20–30, 31–40, 41–50, 51–60) and then testing for association between regulatory focus and selections made on both measures. The logit models indicate no significant results between different age groups and the asset and portfolio selections. Hβ is thus unsupported.

5.3.3 *Validity of Hγ*

Research indicates that education is associated with risk preferences, although with mixed findings (Watson and McNaughton 2007). As regulatory focus is also associated with risk preferences (Kirmani and Zhu 2007), education, regulatory focus and risk preferences may be related. In the context of this book, risk preferences are modelled by financial allocation decisions. To explore Hγ, participants are examined based on their education levels (basic degree, higher degree) and then testing for the association between regulatory focus and selections made on both measures. Significant results are observed for the association between regulatory focus and eye tracker—portfolio, for the higher degree group, but not for the basic degree group. No significant results were obtained for the association between regulatory focus and eye tracker—asset selection, self-report—asset selection or self-report—portfolio selection.

5.3.3.1 Validity of Hγ: Eye Tracker

Table 5.17 indicates that when only participants with a higher degree are included, a chi-square test for the association between regulatory focus and eye tracker—portfolio selection, yields a main effect ($n = 39$, $\chi^2 = 4.837$, $p < 0.05$). Table 5.17 states that 86.7 % of those with a chronic prevention focus spend proportionately more time on the prevention portfolio scenario. For chronic promotion focused participants, there was no observable difference. No significant results were obtained for the basic degree group.

To obtain further insight into the relationship between regulatory focus, eye tracker—portfolio selection and education, a logistic regression was conducted. Eye tracker—portfolio selection was the dependent variable, and age, education, ethnicity, marital status, regulatory focus, financial literacy, gender and regulatory focus * education were the independent variables. The interaction term, regulatory focus * education was added to gain further understanding into the relationship between regulatory focus and gender. Table 5.18, indicates the results.

Table 5.18 indicates that while education is not significant, regulatory focus * education is significant ($\beta = 2.924$, $p < 0.10$). This indicates that those who are prevention-focused and possess a higher degree are more likely to look at the prevention portfolio for a proportionately longer time.

Table 5.17 Basic Pearson chi-squared test and cross tabulation for regulatory focus * eye tracker—portfolio (higher degree)

	Value	df	Asymp. sig. (1-sided)
Pearson chi-square	4.387	1	0.018

		Eye tracker—portfolio		Total
		Promotion	Prevention	
Regulatory focus	Promotion	11	13	24
	Prevention	2	13	15
Total		13	26	39

Table 5.18 Logit model for eye tracker—portfolio selection against age, education, ethnicity, marital status, regulatory focus, financial literacy, gender, regulatory focus * education

Dependent variable	−2 Log likelihood	Cox and Snell R square	Nagelkerke R square
Eye tracker—portfolio selection	102.925	0.153	0.213
Variable	*β*	S.E.	Sig.
Age	−1.013	0.911	0.133
Education	−0.619	1.041	0.276
Ethnicity	−0.941	1.026	0.180
Marital status	0.831	0.771	0.141
Regulatory focus	−1.021	0.657	0.060
Financial literacy	−1.121	0.533	0.018
Gender	0.781	0.521	0.067
Regulatory focus * education	2.924	1.121	0.005
Constant	1.222	0.605	0.022

5.3.4 *Validity of Further Hypotheses: Summary*

Hα is supported by the data, indicated by the associations between regulatory focus and eye tracker—asset selection, regulatory focus and self-report—asset selection, regulatory focus and self-report—portfolio selection. Hβ, however, is unsupported, with no relationship observed between regulatory focus, selections and age. Regarding Hγ, significant results are demonstrated for the association between regulatory focus and eye tracker—portfolio, for the higher degree group, but not for the basic degree group. The section that follows is concerned with additional analyses apart from the hypotheses.

5.4 Additional Analyses

5.4.1 *Asset and Portfolio Selection*

As indicated in Sect. 4.3.2.1, the portfolios provided in the book are not previously tested. This section explores whether the portfolios are associated with states of promotion and prevention. If the assets are associated with the portfolios, it would indicate that the portfolios are sensitive to states of promotion and prevention. Thus, a chi-squared test of association was conducted to determine the association between asset selection and portfolio selection. Significant results were only obtained for the association between self-report—asset selection and self-report—portfolio selection, but not when eye tracker was used as the instrument (eye tracker—asset and eye tracker—portfolio).

Table 5.19 Basic pearson chi-squared test and cross tabulation for portfolio allocation * asset allocation

		Value	df	Asymp. sig. (1-sided)
Pearson chi-square		7.444	1	0.003

		Self-report—asset		Total
		Promotion	Prevention	
Self-report—portfolio	Promotion	28	22	50
	Prevention	12	31	43
Total		40	53	93

Table 5.19 indicates the chi-squared test of association between self-report—asset selection and self-report—portfolio selection, where there was a main effect (n = 93, χ^2 = 7.444, p < 0.05). Table 5.19 indicates that 72.1 % of those who selected the prevention asset selected the prevention portfolio. 56 % of those who selected the promotion asset also selected the promotion portfolio.

5.4.1.1 Asset and Portfolio Selection: Regulatory Focus

Research indicates that regulatory focus is associated with certain assets (Zhou and Pham 2004). The significant results given in the previous section, is likely that examining groups based on the chronic regulatory focus may yield further insight into the relationship between asset and portfolio selections with one's chronic regulatory focus. Significant results were only obtained for the association between self-report—asset selection and self-report—portfolio selection for the chronic promotion-focused, but not for the chronic prevention-focused. No significant results were obtained for the association between eye tracker—asset selection and eye tracker—portfolio selection, after examining participants by their regulatory focus.

Table 5.20 represents the results for the promotion group, with a main effect of self-report—asset selection on self-report—portfolio selection (n = 50, χ^2 = 10.628, p < 0.05). Table 5.20 indicates that 56 % of the promotion participants selected the prevention asset. No significant results were obtained for the prevention group, although the majority of prevention-oriented participants selected the prevention asset. The next section divides participants by their education level (basic degree, higher degree) and tests the association between asset and portfolio selection.

Table 5.20 Basic Pearson chi-squared test and cross tabulation for portfolio allocation * asset allocation (Chronic promotion focus)

		Value	df	Asymp. sig. (1-sided)
Pearson chi-square		10.628	1	0.001

		Self-report—asset		Total
		Promotion	Prevention	
Self-report—portfolio	Promotion	18	10	28
	Prevention	4	18	22
Total		22	28	50

Table 5.21 Basic Pearson chi-squared test and cross tabulation for Portfolio allocation * asset allocation (higher degree)

		Value	df	Asymp. sig. (1-sided)
Pearson chi-square		12.230	1	0.000

		Self-report—asset		Total
		Promotion	Prevention	
Self-report—portfolio	Promotion	14	11	25
	Prevention	0	14	14
Total		14	25	39

5.4.1.2 Asset and Portfolio Selection: Education

In Sect. 5.3.3, education had a significant effect on the portfolio selections made on the eye tracker. Thus, education may have an effect on the relationship between asset and portfolio selection. To gain further insight, participants were examined based on their education level (basic degree, higher degree) and a chi-square test for the association between self-report—asset selection and self-report measure—portfolio selection, eye tracker—asset selection and eye tracker—portfolio selection was conducted. Significant results were only observed for the association between self-report—asset selection and self-report—portfolio selection, for the higher degree group.

Table 5.21 indicates that when only participants in the higher degree group are included, there was a main effect of self-report—asset selection and self-report—portfolio selection ($n = 39$, $\chi^2 = 12.230$, $p < 0.05$). None of those who selected the promotion asset picked the prevention portfolio. Participants had a roughly equal chance of selecting the promotion or prevention portfolio after selecting the prevention asset. As indicated in this section, having a higher degree seems to lead to select only promotion portfolio, after selecting the prevention asset on the self-report. In this section and Sect. 5.3.3, significant results were only obtained for higher degree participants.

5.5 Summary of Results

The main hypotheses were unsupported, regardless of the measure used, be it the eye tracker or self-report. Participants were more likely to select prevention assets, on both the eye tracker and self-report. They were more likely to select prevention portfolios on the eye tracker, but were almost equally likely to select either portfolio on the self-report. The effect of the adverse world financial outlook is purported to have influenced participants, to select the asset and portfolio, not in accordance to their regulatory focus.

Hα and Hγ are supported, indicating that gender and education are related to regulatory focus and the selections made. Hβ was not supported indicating that age may not have had an effect on the relationship at hand. Several other findings were also obtained. The cross tabulations of asset and portfolio selection yielded interesting insights when participants were segmented into their demographic variables. The section that follows discusses the results obtained and puts forth explanations to the various findings observed.

Chapter 6
General Discussion

Abstract This chapter commences with a discussion of the key findings, the validity of the hypotheses and insights from the eye tracking analysis. This is followed by a discussion of the other relevant findings in the experiment.

6.1 Key Findings

6.1.1 Main Hypotheses

Tests of association between one's asset selection decisions and their regulatory focus did not provide any significant results (H1). Neither the self-report nor the eye tracker measure yielded significant results in this aspect. As such, H1 is unsupported, and it is concluded that chronic promotion and prevention-focused participants do not choose promotion and prevention-based assets respectively. On the eye tracker and self-report, participants were more likely to select the prevention asset, regardless of their regulatory focus. It is postulated that this is due to the effect of the unfavourable world financial outlook, causing participants to choose assets that are not associated with chronic regulatory foci.

Concerning H2, tests of association between one's portfolio selection decisions and their regulatory focus did not yield any significant results. Neither the self-report nor the eye tracker measure yielded significant results in this aspect. Thus, H2 is unsupported, and it is concluded that promotion and prevention-focused participants do not choose promotion and prevention-based portfolios respectively. On the self-report, participants were almost equally likely to choose either portfolio, and tended to choose the prevention portfolio on the eye tracker, regardless of their chronic regulatory foci. This was purported to be due to the effect of the harsh world financial outlook, causing participants to choose portfolios that do not match their chronic regulatory foci.

N. Kumar, *Chronic Regulatory Focus and Financial Decision-Making*,
SpringerBriefs in Finance, DOI 10.1007/978-981-287-694-2_6

It may be argued that participants were more likely to select the prevention-based assets on the eye tracker and self-report and the prevention portfolio on the eye tracker because of the high proportion of Asians, possibly culturally biased to being more risk averse. However, as stated in Sect. 4.3.1.2, participants would be made aware of various modes of thought by virtue of studying at a highly ranked cosmopolitan university, negating the effects of inherent risk preferences.

Research states that when hypotheses are unsupported, it may be due to imprecise research (Grant 1962) and that if statistically significant results are obtained, only then it is certain that the experiment was done properly (Festinger 1953; Wilson and Miller 1964). However, such a viewpoint disregards useful insights that may arise from unsupported hypotheses. Guidelines have been set for acceptance of the unsupported hypotheses; testing many subjects, controlling for variance, having sensitive measurements and avoiding floor and ceiling effects (Frick 1995). Though most of these criteria require subjective judgments (Frick 1995), this book addresses the issues successfully.

Simply put, the attempt to demonstrate a statistically significant effect, but fail, is the only way to give credence to an unsupported hypothesis (Frick 1995). In this book, the researcher set out to validate the hypotheses, but was unable to do so, and thus proposed an alternative explanation. The next section provides some explanation for the unsupported main hypotheses.

6.1.1.1 Financial Outlook

Past studies indicate that placing a warning concerning faked responses, before personality tests, can result in decreased average scores (Dwight and Donovan 2003). In addition, instruction sets and other similar manipulations can alter personality tests (Nordlund and Snell 2006). These influences, whilst subtle, have strong effects concerning a variety of outcomes (Nordlund 2009). Most relevant to this study, is that such effects can modify behaviour, such as making one more polite or rude (Bargh et al. 1996), even facilitating new characteristics (DeMarree et al. 2005). It is also known that environmental factors non-associated with experiment results can influence outcomes (Matthey 2010).

Thus, it is proposed that the effect of the adverse world financial climate acted as an external, uncontrollable influence, causing most participants to select assets and portfolios that were not in accordance with their regulatory foci. Given that the unfavourable world financial outlook constantly surrounds the participant, its effect may be far longer and salient than effects induced in controlled experimental settings. This effect is proposed to be similar to external primes, which are peripheral and guide one to certain sections of information (Morris 2012). Thus, the external effect of the financial crisis has possibly acted as an external influence, overcoming the effect of respondent's chronic regulatory focus.

This is unsurprising as after the 1987 crash, for example, many investors were still nervous about the market, even after the recovery (Butterworth 1989). It has been noted that a decline in stock prices leads to a decline in consumer confidence, even with households that did not own stock (Garner 1988), which may explain why the majority of participants selected the prevention asset. Investors' behaviour is affected by social movements (Shiller et al. 1984), and thus if the majority is of the opinion that the economy is poor, most people would tend to err on the side of caution and look to less risky, prevention-associated assets. After the recent crisis, individual behaviour is altered, influenced by the environment. Consumers buy cheaper goods and eat out less (Gärling et al. 2009; Association for Psychological Science 2010) and experience reductions in spending behaviour even years after (Naghi et al. 2015). Some also choose to reallocate financial assets (Essner and Rosenius 2012). Overall, there exists much literature on how firms react in hard times (Bloom et al. 2001, 2007; Carruth et al. 2000), but there have been minimal studies on how the average consumer behaves in a poor economic climate (Gärling et al. 2009).

At present, seminal studies in priming (Bargh et al. 1996; Dijksterhuis and Van Knippenberg 1998) are facing controversy, as recent studies have failed to replicate findings (Doyen et al. 2012; Pashler et al. 2012; Shanks et al. 2013; Yong 2012). Although methods have been proposed to remedy the situation (Kahneman 2012), the antecedents for the lack of replicability have not been considered. It may be that stronger, more immersive effects, such as the harsh world financial climate may outplay the effects of priming in controlled experimental conditions. The effect of such external effects may be the cause of the lack of replicability of various priming studies. This research postulates that when inducing primes in experiments related to financial decision-making, the researcher must take into account the effects of events such as financial crises. These black swan (Taleb 2010) events are likely to have an effect on the results, regardless of any primes induced within the experiment. In the context of this study, it is put forward that the effect of the poor financial environment overrode the participants' chronic regulatory focus. Whilst regulatory focus may guide how one pursues goals, it appears that the financial climate has a far greater influence on one's decisions. The next section explores the additional hypotheses put forth.

6.1.2 Further Hypotheses

6.1.2.1 Hα

The results in Sect. 5.3.1 indicate that on the self-report measure, female prevention-focused participants are more likely to select prevention assets, and female promotion-focused participants are more likely to select the promotion portfolio. No significant results were obtained for males. Research indicates that gender is not associated with regulatory focus (Dholakia et al. 2006; Förster et al. 1998;

Keller 2006; Lee et al. 2000). However, the data indicates significant results for the association between gender and regulatory focus. It is possible that gender may be related to regulatory focus, only in the context for financial decision-making, as the different genders make financial decisions differently (Powell and Ansic 1997).

6.1.2.2 Hβ

The hypothesis concerning the relationship between regulatory focus and age did not yield significant results. However, as risk preferences tend to shift with age (Agarwal et al. 2007) and regulatory focus is linked with the former, further study may be required in this aspect.

6.1.2.3 Hγ

As the study was conducted in a university, the participants who indicated that they had a higher degree are academics. In Sect. 5.3.3, on the self-report, none of the academics selected the promotion asset and then the prevention portfolio thereafter, and of those who had chosen the prevention asset, had an equal chance of selecting the promotion or prevention portfolio.

The majority of the academics had a chronic promotion focus. The participants who had a basic degree (non-academics) were equally likely to have either foci. Self-actualisation (Maslow et al. 1970) indicates that academics are motivated by the opportunity for scientific contribution, autonomy (Rowley 1996) and the status achieved in their vocation (Erez and Shneorson 1980). Such traits are similar to the promotion focus on aspiration and accomplishments (Liberman et al. 1999). It may be that a chronic promotion focus is typical of academics. On the self-report, none of the academics chose the promotion asset and the prevention portfolio thereafter. This may be because academics who selected the promotion asset are primarily risk seeking and would thus not select the more conservative prevention portfolio.

Significant results were obtained for those who possess a higher degree (Master's degree and above) for both the eye tracker (Sect. 5.3.2) and self-report (Sect. 5.3.3), but not for those who possess a basic degree. Those who are better educated tend to be more active in financial markets (Cole and Shastry 2009), and it is proposed that those who have a basic degree are unfamiliar with the financial products used. Thus, this may explain the non-significant results for the basic degree participants. Selecting participants with a basic degree was necessary to ensure a robust and diverse sample (Sect. 4.3.1). Overall, there has been little research on the relationship between education and financial decision-making and further study is necessary to gain greater insight. The next section brings together all the results observed on the eye tracker, and compares them with the results obtained on the self-report.

6.2 Eye Tracker Selections

This section discusses the conclusions drawn from the eye tracker results. Although both the eye tracker and self-report were complementary instruments to determine asset and portfolio allocations, both these selections do not necessarily match, i.e. those who select a prevention asset on the eye tracker may not select the prevention asset on the self-report. It is postulated that eye tracker may give insights into the type of information viewed by consumers, but does not provide clear indication of whether this information was used to make the associated financial decision on the self-report.

As in Sect. 5.3.1, females are more likely to look at the prevention asset for a proportionately longer time, compared to male participants. Research indicates that women are more financially risk averse than men (Bernasek and Shwiff 2001; Jianakoplos and Bernasek 1998; Olsen and Cox 2001) and that prevention focused individuals make more conservative investments (Kirmani and Zhu 2007). It is thus hypothesised that females would spend more time looking at the prevention-associated, less risky asset, due to their risk averse nature (Jianakoplos and Bernasek 1998).

In Sect. 5.3.2, those who are prevention focused and possess a higher degree are more likely to look at the prevention portfolio for a proportionately longer time. Knowledge acquired from formal schooling improves credit scores and reduces the probability of declaring bankruptcy (Cole et al. 2012). This may indicate that education results in more cautious and risk-averse behaviour. The effect of one's chronic prevention focus, linked to the preference of conservative investments (Kirmani and Zhu 2007), and education level may work in tandem to give rise to risk-averse behaviour, explaining why higher educated participants who are prevention-focused look at the less risky prevention-associated portfolio for a proportionately longer period of time.

As in Sects. 5.2.1 and 5.2.3, those who scored poorly on the financial literacy test were less likely to look at the prevention asset and portfolio for a proportionately longer time. It is known that those who have low financial literacy are less likely to invest in the stock market (Rooij et al. 2007), and would thus be unfamiliar with stock. As such, they would be drawn to look at the riskier asset (stock) and portfolio that they are unfamiliar with, for a proportionately longer amount of time. It must be noted that the financial literacy test in this book was more of a check to make sure that the original screening for financial literacy was effective, rather than an actual measure of financial literacy. Thus, further analysis into the financial literacy variable was not conducted.

As indicated in Sect. 5.2.1, participants who are prevention focused are less likely to look at the prevention asset for a proportionately longer time, compared to promotion-focused participants. It may be that the chronic prevention-focused participants' thought process is reflected in their likelihood to spend proportionately more time on the promotion asset. This may be due to their emphasis on accuracy (Pham and Chang 2010) and need to avoid mismatches to their goals, considering only clearly suitable choices (Zhu and Meyers-Levy 2007).

6.2.1 *Decision-Making Process*

Academics are divided with regard to whether eye movement reflects one's mental processes and subsequent decisions. Certain research indicates that eye movements reflect the thought process (Lohse 1997) but other studies indicate that resulting fixation patterns may not indicate one's attention, only where the eye has been viewing (Wright and Ward 2008). This book provides support for the view that eye tracking may not necessarily imply a corresponding thought process.

In this book, the eye tracker and self-report measure were instruments to determine the asset and portfolio selections of participants. The eye tracking results indicate that while participants may look proportionately longer at certain assets or portfolios, they may not select the same item on the self-report measure. It is postulated that the eye tracker may give insights into the type of information viewed by participants, but does not provide strong indication of whether this information was used to make an associated financial decision. It is necessary to use the eye tracker in tandem with more advanced devices, such as the fMRI[1] and EEG.[2] These devices, along with the eye tracker, will provide a deeper understanding of the processes that lead to one's related financial decision.

6.3 Other Findings

Apart from the hypotheses that were discussed in the previous section, several other findings were also observed. They will be discussed in the following section.

6.3.1 *Chronic Prevention Focus*

In Sect. 5.3.1, on the self-report, females are less likely than males to select the prevention rather than the promotion portfolio, but this effect is weaker for females who have a chronic prevention orientation. The chronic prevention focus appears to cause females to be more likely to select prevention portfolios, with no significant results obtained for the chronic promotion-focused females.

In Sect. 5.3.4, chronic promotion-focused participants who reported a positive outlook only selected the prevention asset on the self-report. Previous research indicates that the prevention system yields results in certain controlled situations,

---

[1]fMRI (Functional magnetic resonance imaging) is a procedure that measures brain activity by detecting associated changes in blood flow.

[2]In this case, the EEG (Electroencephalography) refers to the device that records electrical activity along the scalp. The EEG measures voltage fluctuations resulting from ionic current flow within the neurons of the brain.

with no observable results for the promotion system (Scholer et al. 2010). It appears that the chronic prevention system is stronger than the effect of one's positive world outlook. However, it must be noted that the participants who reported a positive financial outlook is minimal. While it can be hypothesised that the chronic prevention system is stronger than the chronic promotion system, further study is required before any clear conclusions can be drawn.

6.3.2 *Asset and Portfolio Selection*

On the self-report, most of the participants who selected the promotion asset selected the promotion portfolio, and most of those who selected the prevention asset selected the prevention portfolio. It is already known that the assets in the book are associated with different regulatory foci (Zhou and Pham 2004). Given that the portfolios are associated with the assets, it is proposed that they are sensitive to one's regulatory focus. However, not all variables give significant results for both the eye tracker and self-report. The results suggest the need to include more sophisticated instruments such as the EEG or fMRI.

6.3.3 *Distraction Scenario*

The distraction scenario used in the experiment was to prevent participants from determining the hypotheses (Shavit et al. 2010). Participants were asked to 'write about what happened yesterday' and were given a whole page to do so. Upon sorting the completed distraction scenario according to participants' chronic regulatory foci, clear differences were observed between the writing styles of the chronic promotion and prevention participants. There has been little study on the writing styles particular to one's regulatory focus, although there exist several studies linking personality to writing style (Argamon et al. 2005; Wolfradt and Pretz 2001). Future studies should analyse the writing samples of chronic promotion and prevention participants to gain greater insight into their differing writing styles.

6.3.4 *Ethnicity*

Previous studies indicate that the promotion and prevention system are more chronically accessible for those from individualist and collectivist cultures respectively (Lee et al. 2000). Studies also indicate that those from a collectivist background are more risk seeking than those from an individualist background (Hsee and Weber 1999; Weber and Hsee 1998). However, no significant results were obtained with regard to a chi-squared test of association between ethnicity and regulatory focus. It is postulated that this is due to the book being conducted in a cosmopolitan university. In a university with people of diverse backgrounds, participants would be exposed to modes of thought that are different to their own, and this is proposed to mitigate the effect of one's background predicating their risk preferences and chronic regulatory focus. A cosmopolitan university environment, located in an Asian country, did not give rise to an overwhelming number of prevention participants, although most are from collectivist cultural backgrounds. Instead, there was a roughly even split between chronic promotion and chronic prevention participants.

6.3.5 Theory

The change in risk appetite for financial products, depending on the stimuli presented, is proposed by Zhou and Pham (2004). This book proposes that external stimuli, such as the adverse world financial outlook, can also cause one to select different assets than one normally would.

In the Scholer et al. (2010) study, when a risky option offered the sole possibility of returning to the status quo, after a loss, prevention motivation predicted risk seeking, but no significant results were obtained for the promotion system. Similarly, in this book, those who possessed a prevention focus selected the prevention asset on the self-report, even after reporting a positive outlook. For the promotion system, there were no significant results. However, further study is necessary to draw a conclusion with regard to the relative strength of the prevention system over the promotion system.

This book highlights the importance of understanding the motivations that drive financial decision-making. These motivations are purported to explain much of the phenomena that underlie behavioural finance. It is hoped that the extensions to theory proposed by this book, highlight the importance of psychological theory in contemporary financial research. The next section concludes the book and indicates the limitations observed, along with future directions for research.

Chapter 7
Conclusion

Abstract This chapter begins with a brief summary of the results, followed by the limitations and opportunities for future research. A section on the concluding statements then bookends the thesis.

7.1 Summary of Results

The main hypotheses were unsupported, and chronic regulatory focus had no significant effect on asset or portfolio allocation. This was postulated to be due to the influence of the unfavourable world financial outlook, which caused participants to select assets and portfolios unrelated to their chronic regulatory focus. Regarding the further hypotheses, Hα and Hγ were supported, indicating that gender and education are associated with regulatory focus and asset and portfolio decisions. The data does not support Hβ and it may be that age was not related to regulatory focus and asset and portfolio decisions, although further study may be necessary in this aspect.

Eye tracking is deemed to give insight into how participants make financial decisions, but does not provide a clear indication of whether this information was used to make the associated financial decision on the self-report. Several other findings were reported, which provide opportunities for future research, as denoted in Sect. 7.3.

7.2 Limitations

Given its exploratory nature, this book has several limitations, which are important in outlining, so as to pioneer future research.

Whether eye movements represent one's thoughts or otherwise are still is not certain. Eye tracking is proposed to give insight into how participants make financial decisions, but does not provide an accurate indication of whether this

N. Kumar, *Chronic Regulatory Focus and Financial Decision-Making*,
SpringerBriefs in Finance, DOI 10.1007/978-981-287-694-2_7

information was used to make the related financial choice on the self-report. As stated in the preceding chapter, advanced devices such as the fMRI or EEG may be used in tandem to give further understanding into one's decision-making process.

Unlike the assets used in this book, the portfolios are not empirically tested to be sensitive to one's regulatory focus. Although the portfolios selected are associated with the asset choices, further empirical testing is necessary. From this process, the portfolios may be modified and aligned closer to the tenets of regulatory focus theory.

This book was conducted in an Asian country, but at an Australian university. The term 'Mutual funds' is not commonly used in Australia, and the Australian academics who participated in the research were thus excluded. Future studies will ensure that all assets and portfolios used are familiar to participants of varying nationalities, especially in universities where there are staff and students of different nationalities. Given the exploratory nature of the study, the limitations observed can provide avenues for future research, and were explored in the following section.

7.3 Future Directions

From a theoretical standpoint, this book has shown that chronic regulatory focus may not always be the system that drives one's financial decision-making. This book hopes to encourage more research in finance, involving regulatory focus theory. As this work is of an exploratory nature, much of the results herein are more directions for future research rather than conclusions on their own. This section will briefly summarise the key findings that can pioneer future research.

The adverse world financial outlook is proposed to have influenced the participants, causing them to select assets and portfolios not in accordance to their regulatory foci. It appears that the poor world financial climate is far greater an influence than one's chronic regulatory focus. The exact mechanism of the effect requires further study. Most of the participants selected the more conservative, prevention-associated assets on the self-report, postulated to be due to the effect of the negative financial outlook. To the best of the researcher's knowledge, there has been no research on how the average consumer shifts their investment patterns when the economic climate worsens. Such research can be of use to financial institutions, to aid in their marketing processes during unfavourable economic times.

Previous research does not explore how participants can be influenced by such exogenous factors, such as a poor economic climate. Future studies can explore how major world events influence participants to make decisions that are not in accordance with their chronic regulatory focus. For example, those who have experienced a natural disaster, may be influenced to make decisions that are prevention associated, irrespective of their original chronic regulatory focus. Such research may be useful in tailoring policy decisions for those affected in such a way.

On the self-report, females who were prevention-focused were more likely to select the prevention asset, and females who were promotion-focused were more likely to select the promotion portfolio. Previous research indicates no association between gender and regulatory focus. It may be that for financial decision-making, gender is related to regulatory focus. Further study can be conducted in this area, to determine if regulatory focus is contingent on gender, in the context of financial decision-making.

The majority of the academics who participated in the experiment had a chronic promotion focus, which was linked to previous studies on the motivations of the former. Further study can be done to confirm whether certain occupations predicate the necessity for a certain regulatory foci. This will aid firms in their hiring and career planning processes, better matching applicants to occupations most suited to their regulatory foci.

Those who had a chronic prevention focus, and a positive outlook still selected the prevention asset on the self-report. However, this book had very few participants reporting a positive financial outlook, given the harsh economic climate. Future study can be done on a far greater scale, so as to recruit a large number of participants with a positive outlook. The aim of such a study would be to research the relative strength of the prevention system, over the promotion system. If financial institutions are able to determine the chronic regulatory focus of their participants before marketing financial products, detailed information on both systems would aid in specifically tailoring products to cater for such individuals.

The data indicates that the eye tracking selections do not significantly match the selections indicated on the self-report. It was proposed that the eye tracker selections may give insights into the type of information viewed by consumers but does not provide clear indication of whether this information was used to make an associated financial decision on the self-report. As the eye tracker cannot determine one's actual thought process, more advanced devices should be used in tandem, such as the EEG and fMRI, and a similar experiment conducted. At present, there are limited studies involving the EEG/fMRI and financial decision-making (Knutson and Bossaerts 2007; Kuhnen and Knutson 2005), and future studies in this area would give insight into how individuals make financial decisions.

On the self-report, most of the participants who selected the promotion asset also selected the promotion portfolio, and most of those who selected the prevention asset also selected the prevention portfolio. This indicates that the portfolios provided for this experiment are reflective of states of promotion and prevention. Further study can empirically test whether participants select promotion or prevention portfolios after having been primed for a promotion or prevention condition. Such research will aid financial institutions, and enable them to cater to their customer's regulatory foci when marketing financial products.

The individuals taking part in this research are presumably made more aware of how they choose various financial products, and their inherent biases, if any. Participants, from knowing their own chronic regulatory focus, may put more thought into selecting financial products, regardless of the world financial situation. For policy makers, it may be possible for future financial literacy frameworks to take into account one's chronic regulatory focus, catering more effectively to individual needs. The next section provides the conclusion for this book, highlighting the key findings observed.

7.4 Concluding Statements

The primary purpose of this book is to see if chronic regulatory focus is associated with certain assets and portfolios. However, the main hypotheses indicate that there is no significant association between one's chronic regulatory focus and their asset and portfolio selection. It was proposed that the effect of the unfavourable world financial outlook caused most participants selecting the prevention asset on both measures, and the prevention portfolio on the eye tracker. Overall, participants did not choose assets or portfolios that were associated with their chronic regulatory focus. The additional hypotheses indicate that education and gender are related to regulatory focus and asset and portfolio allocation, whilst age does not appear to share a similar association.

Although participants looked at certain assets and portfolios for a proportionately longer time, they did not necessarily select these assets or portfolios on the self-report. Thus, eye tracking may give insights into the type of information viewed by consumers but does not provide a clear indication if this information was actually used to make an associated financial decision. Future research should consider using more advanced devices in tandem with the eye tracker to gain further insight into consumer decision-making process.

Overall, this study is of an exploratory nature, and much of the findings in this book suggest the possibility of future studies in both finance and consumer behaviour. Possible policy implications and improved marketing processes for financial institutions are the intended outcomes for this research. For the participants involved in the experiment, it is hoped that they will gain a greater understanding of the underlying processes that lead to their financial decisions. It is also expected that individuals will be able to make financial decisions that are not hampered by their own inherent biases, and select those which are most appropriate for their risk appetite and prevailing economic situation.

This research ties together concepts from finance and psychology, to gain insight into how financial decisions are made. Future research in this vein will be of great importance to both areas, increasing the depth of both fields, aiding in the easing of psychological theories into the mainstream of financial research, augmenting the ability of financial theory in explaining financial outcomes.

Appendix

A.1 Composite Regulatory Focus Scale

Please indicate your response by circling the number which most reflects you

No.	Questions	Not at all true of me						Very true of me
1	When it comes to achieving things that are important to me, I find that I don't perform as well as I would ideally like to do	1	2	3	4	5	6	7
2	I feel like I have made progress toward being successful in my life	1	2	3	4	5	6	7
3	When I see an opportunity for something I like, I get excited right away	1	2	3	4	5	6	7
4	I frequently imagine how I will achieve my hopes and aspirations	1	2	3	4	5	6	7
5	I see myself as someone who is primarily striving to reach my "ideal self"—to fulfill my hopes, wishes, and aspirations	1	2	3	4	5	6	7
6	I usually obeyed rules and regulations that were established by my parents	1	2	3	4	5	6	7
7	Not being careful enough has gotten me into trouble at times	1	2	3	4	5	6	7
8	I worry about making mistakes	1	2	3	4	5	6	7
9	I frequently think about how I can prevent failures in my life	1	2	3	4	5	6	7
10	I see myself as someone who is primarily striving to become the self I "ought" to be—fulfill my duties, responsibilities and obligations	1	2	3	4	5	6	7

N. Kumar, *Chronic Regulatory Focus and Financial Decision-Making*,
SpringerBriefs in Finance, DOI 10.1007/978-981-287-694-2

A.2 Distraction Scenario

Write about what happened yesterday.

A.3 Allocation Situations

Imagine you have $6000 available and can allocate it in either one of the two groups of assets, as below. In which group would you put more of your funds? Indicate your selection, via a tick in the box below.	
Stocks	**Mutual Funds**

<table>
<tr><td colspan="2">Imagine you have $6000 available and can allocate it in
either one of the two portfolios, as below.
In which group would you put more of your funds?
Both portfolios account for inflation
Indicate your selection, via a tick in the box below.</td></tr>
<tr><th>Option A</th><th>Option B</th></tr>
<tr><td>High gains, and possible losses, may not maintain value over time</td><td>No gains, and no losses, will maintain value over time</td></tr>
<tr><td></td><td></td></tr>
</table>

A.4 Surveys of Consumers

Specific questions have drawn from this survey, as follows:

1. The earlier you start saving for retirement, the more money you will have because the effects of compound interest increase over time.
   True/False

2. A stock mutual fund combines the money of many investors to buy a variety of stocks.
   True/False

3. Over the long term, stocks have the highest rate of return on money invested.
   True/False

4. Mutual funds pay a guaranteed rate of return.
   True/False

   The correct answers have been underlined.

A.5 Complete Questionnaire

Dear Respondent

The following questions are to find out about your predispositions and how they can affect decisions you make. Completing the questionnaire should not take more than 15 minutes. Thank you for your time.

Gender:	Age:			Marital status:	Highest qualification:
		20-30			
		31-40			
		41-50			
		51-60			
		61-70			

Please indicate your response by circling the number which most reflects you

No.	Questions	Not at all true of me						Very true of me
1	When it comes to achieving things that are important to me, I find that I don't perform as well as I would ideally like to do	1	2	3	4	5	6	7
2	I feel like I have made progress toward being successful in my life	1	2	3	4	5	6	7
3	When I see an opportunity for something I like, I get excited right away	1	2	3	4	5	6	7
4	I frequently imagine how I will achieve my hopes and aspirations	1	2	3	4	5	6	7
5	I see myself as someone who is primarily striving to reach my "ideal self"—to fulfill my hopes, wishes, and aspirations	1	2	3	4	5	6	7
6	I usually obey rules and regulations that were established by my parents	1	2	3	4	5	6	7

(continued)

(continued)

No.	Questions	Not at all true of me						Very true of me
7	Not being careful enough has gotten me into trouble at times	1	2	3	4	5	6	7
8	I worry about making mistakes	1	2	3	4	5	6	7
9	I frequently think about how I can prevent failures in my life	1	2	3	4	5	6	7
10	I see myself as someone who is primarily striving to become the self I "ought" to be—fulfill my duties, responsibilities and obligations	1	2	3	4	5	6	7

Write about what happened yesterday

Imagine you have $6000 available and can allocate it in either one of the two groups of assets, as below. In which group would you put more of your funds? Indicate your selection, via a tick in the box below.	
Stocks	**Mutual Funds**

Imagine you have $6000 available and can allocate it in either one of the two portfolios, as below. In which group would you put more of your funds? **Both portfolios account for inflation** Indicate your selection, via a tick in the box below.	
Option A	**Option B**
High gains, and possible losses, may not maintain value over time	No gains, and no losses, will maintain value over time

Please circle the relevant 'True' or 'False'

1. The earlier you start saving for retirement, the more money you will have because the effects of compounding interest increase over time.
   True/False

2. A stock mutual fund combines the money of many investors to buy a variety of stocks.
   True/False

3. Over the long term, stocks have the highest rate of return on money invested.
   True/False

4. Mutual funds pay a guaranteed rate of return.
   True/False

What do you feel about the current global financial situation?

References

Aaker JL, Lee AY (2001) "I" seek pleasures and "we" avoid pains: the role of self-regulatory goals in information processing and persuasion. J Consum Res 28(1):33–49
Aaker JL, Lee AY (2006) Understanding regulatory fit. J Mark Res 43(1):15–19
Abraham A, Ikenberry DL (1994) The individual investor and the weekend effect. J Financ Quant Anal 29(2):263–277
Agarwal S, Driscoll JC, Gabaix X, Laibson D (2007) The age of reason: financial decisions over the lifecycle. (Working paper no. 13191). National Bureau of Economic Research. Retrieved from https://www.nber.org/papers/w13191.pdf
Anderson LR, Gerlach JR, DiTraglia FJ (2007) Yes, wall street, there is a january effect! Evidence from laboratory auctions. J Behav Financ 8(1):1–8
Argamon S, Dhawle S, Koppel M, Pennebaker J (2005) Lexical predictors of personality type. Paper presented at the joint annual meeting of the interface and the classification society of North America.
Ariel RA (1990) High stock returns before holidays: existence and evidence on possible causes. J Financ 45(5):1611–1626
Aronson E (1991) The social animal, vol 6. W.H. Freeman, New York, NY
Association for Psychological Science. (2010). The psychology of financial decision making and economic crises. Retrieved 9 June 2015, from http://www.sciencedaily.com/releases/2010/09/100922111428.htm
Avnet T, Higgins ET (2006) How regulatory fit affects value in consumer choices and opinions. J Mark Res 43(1):1–10
Bailard TE, Biehl DL, Kaiser RW (1986) Personal money management, vol 5. Science Research Associates Inc, Chicago
Baker M, Wurgler J (2007) Investor sentiment in the stock market. J Econ Perspect 21(2):129–151
Baker M, Wurgler J (2013) Behavioral corporate finance: an updated survey. Handbook of the economics of finance: Elsevier B.V.
Baker M, Wurgler J, Yuan Y (2012) Global, local, and contagious investor sentiment. J Financ Econ 104(2):272–287
Barber BM, Odean T (2000) Trading is hazardous to your wealth: the common stock investment performance of individual investors. J Financ 55(2):773–806
Barberis N, Xiong W (2009) What drives the disposition effect? An analysis of a long-standing preference-based explanation. J Financ 64(2):751–784
Bargh JA, Chen M, Burrows L (1996) Automaticity of social behavior: direct effects of trait construct and stereotype activation on action. J Pers Soc Psychol 71(2):230
Barnewall MM (1987) Psychological characteristics of the individual investor. In: Droms W (ed) asset allocation for the individual investor charlottesville. VA, The Institute of Chartered Financial Analysts

N. Kumar, *Chronic Regulatory Focus and Financial Decision-Making*,
SpringerBriefs in Finance, DOI 10.1007/978-981-287-694-2

Barsky RB, Juster FT, Kimball MS, Shapiro MD (1997) Preference parameters and behavioral heterogeneity: an experimental approach in the health and retirement study. Q J Econ 112 (2):537–579

Beal D, Delpachitra S (2003) Financial literacy among Australian university students'. Econ Pap 22(1):65–78

Beltramini RF (1983) Student surrogates in consumer research. J Acad Mark Sci 11(4):438–443

Bernartzi S, Thaler RH (1995) Myopic loss aversion and the equity premium puzzle. Q J Econ 110 (1):73–92

Bernasek A, Shwiff S (2001) Gender, risk, and retirement. J Econ Issues 35(2):345–356

Berument H, Kiymaz H (2001) The day of the week effect on stock market volatility. J Econ Financ 25(2):181–193

Bhandari M, Joensson A (2009) Clinical research for surgeons. Thieme

Bloom N, Bond S, Van Reenen J (2001) The dynamics of investment under uncertainty, no. W01/05. Institute for Fiscal Studies

Bloom N, Bond S, Van Reenen J (2007) Uncertainty and investment dynamics. Rev Econ Stud 74 (2):391–415

Boldero JM, Higgins ET (2011) Regulatory focus and political decision making: when people favor reform over the status quo. Polit Psychol 32(3):399–418

Bouman S, Jacobsen B (2002) The halloween indicator, "sell in may and go away": another puzzle. Am Econ Rev 92(5):1618–1635

Brockner J, Paruchuri S, Idson LC, Higgins ET (2002) Regulatory focus and the probability estimates of conjunctive and disjunctive events. Organ Behav Hum Decis Process 87(1):5–24

Brown JR, Coile CC, Weisbenner SJ (2010) The effect of inheritance receipt on retirement. Rev Econ Stat 92(2):425–434

Brunnermeier MK (2001) Preface asset pricing under asymmetric information: bubbles, crashes, technical analysis and herding. Oxford University Press

Butterworth V (1989) After the fall—investing in uncertain times. Bottom Line Managing Libr Financ 2(3):41–42

Calder BJ, Phillips LW, Tybout AM (1981) Designing research for application. J Consum Res 8 (2):197–207

Camacho CJ, Higgins ET, Luger L (2003) Moral value transfer from regulatory fit: What feels right is right and what feels wrong is wrong. J Pers Soc Psychol 84(3):498–510

Carruth A, Dickerson A, Henley A (2000) What do we know about investment under uncertainty? J Econ Surv 14(2):119–154

Carver CS, Scheier MF (1998) On the self-regulation of behavior. Cambridge University Press, New York

Chan C (2012) Effect of a coach's regulatory focus and an individual's implicit person theory on individual performance. J Manage 38(3):809–835

Chen Y, Sun Y (2003) Age differences in financial decision-making: using simple heuristics. Educ Gerontol 29(7):627–635

Chernev A (2004) Goal-attribute compatibility in consumer choice. J Consum Psychol 14(1): 141–150

Chkioua DH, Abaoub E (2012) Home bias in equity portfolios: theory and evidence for developed markets. Int J Econ Financ 4(6)

Ciccone SJ (2011) Investor optimism, false hopes and the January effect. J Behav Financ 12 (3):158–168

Cole S, Shastry GK (2009) Smart money: the effect of education, cognitive ability, and financial literacy on financial market participation. Harvard Business School

Cole S, Paulson A, Shastry G (2012) Smart money: the effect of education on financial behavior. Harvard Bus Sch Financ Working Pap (09-071).

Cooper I, Kaplanis E (1994) The implications of the home bias in equity portfolios. Bus Strategy Rev 5(2):41–53

Cooper MJ, Gulen H, Rau PR (2005) Changing names with style: mutual fund name changes and their effects on fund flows. J Financ 60(6):2825–2858

Crowe E, Higgins E (1997) Regulatory focus and strategic inclinations: promotion and prevention in decision-making. Organ Behav Hum Decis Process 69(2):117–132

Cull M, Whitton D (2011) University students' financial literacy levels: obstacles and aids. Econ Labour Relat Rev 22(1):99–114

Das G (2015) Retail shopping behaviour: understanding the role of regulatory focus theory. Int Rev Retail Distrib Consum Res 1–15

DeMarree KG, Wheeler SC, Petty RE (2005) Priming a new identity: self-monitoring moderates the effects of nonself primes on self-judgments and behavior. J Pers Soc Psychol 89(5):657

Devenow A, Welch I (1996) Rational herding in financial economics. Eur Econ Rev 40(3): 603–615

Dhar R, Zhu N (2002) Up close and personal: an individual level analysis of the disposition effect. Yale ICF Working Paper, No. 02-20.

Dholakia UM, Gopinath M, Bagozzi RP, Nataraajan R (2006) The role of regulatory focus in the experience and self-control of desire for temptations. J Consum Psychol 16(2):163–175

Dichev ID, Janes TD (2003) Lunar cycle effects in stock returns. J Private Equity 6(4):8–29

Dijksterhuis A, Van Knippenberg A (1998) The relation between perception and behavior, or how to win a game of trivial pursuit. J Pers Soc Psychol 74(4):865

Dimotakis N (2012) Team structure and regulatory focus: the impact of regulatory fit on team dynamic. J Appl Psychol 97(2):421–434

Dowling M, Lucey BM (2005) Are weather induced moods priced in global equity markets? Available at SSRN 805944

Doyen S, Klein O, Pichon C-L, Cleeremans A (2012) Behavioral priming: it's all in the mind, but whose mind? PloS one 7(1):e29081

Duchowski AT (2007) Eye tracking methodology: theory and practice, 2nd edn. Springer, London

Dwight SA, Donovan JJ (2003) Do warnings not to fake reduce faking? Hum Perform 16(1):1–23

Edmans A, García D, Norli Ø (2007) Sports sentiment and stock returns. J Financ 62(4):1967–1998

Edward M, Saunders J (1993) Stock prices and wall street weather. Am Econ Rev 83(5): 1337–1345

Egger M, Smith GD, Schneider M, Minder C (1997) Bias in meta-analysis detected by a simple, graphical test. BMJ 315(7109):629–634

Elliot WB (2006) Are investors influenced by pro-forma emphasis and reconciliations in earnings announcements? Account Rev 81(1):113–133

Enis BM, Cox KK, Stafford JE (1972) Students as subjects in consumer behavior experiments. Journal of Marketing Research 9(1):72–74

Erez M, Shneorson Z (1980) Personality types and motivational characteristics of academics versus professionals in industry in the same occupational discipline. J Vocat Behav 17(1): 95–105

Essner N, Rosenius N (2012) The financial crisis effects on asset allocation—a study regarding the individuals in Umeå financial behaviour in response to the financial crisis of 2008. Umeå School of Business and Economics, Umeå, Sweden. Retrieved from http://www.diva-portal.org/smash/get/diva2:600778/FULLTEXT02.pdf

Fama EF (1965) The behaviour of stock market prices. J Bus 38(1):34–105

Fehle F, Tsyplakov S, Zdorovtsov V (2005) Can companies influence investor behaviour through advertising? Super bowl commercials and stock returns. Eur Financ Manage 11(5):625–647

Festinger L (1953) Research methods in the behavioral sciences. In: Festinger L, Katz D (eds) Laboratory experiments. Holt, New York

Field A (2009) Discovering statistics using SPSS, vol 3. Sage Publications, London

Filbeck G, Hatfield P, Horvath P (2005) Risk aversion and personality type. J Behav Financ 6 (4):170–180

Finch J, Mason J (2000) Passing on: kinship and inheritance in England. Routledge, London

Fisher RJ (1993) Social desirability bias and the validity of indirect questioning. J Consum Res 20(2):303–315
Fisher GS (2010). How to profit when efficient markets are driven by inefficient people Retrieved 15 Sept 2013, from http://www.forbes.com/2010/02/08/momentum-stock-investing-personal-finance-gerstein-fisher.html
Florack A, Friese M, Scarabis M (2010) Regulatory focus and reliance on implicit preferences in consumption contexts. J Consum Psychol 20(2):193–204
Floros C, Tan Y (2013) Moon phases, mood and stock market returns: international evidence. J Emerg Market Financ 12(1):107–127
Foad HS (2012) Equity home bias and the euro. Q J Financ 2(1):4–29
Förster J, Higgins ET, Idson LC (1998) Approach and avoidance strength during goal attainment: regulatory focus and the "goal looms larger" effect. J Pers Soc Psychol 75(5):1115
Förster J, Grant H, Idson LC, Higgins ET (2001) Success/failure feedback, expectancies, and approach/avoidance motivation: How regulatory focus moderates classic relations. J Exp Soc Psychol 37(3):253–260
Fox J, Bartholomae S, Lee J (2005) Building the case for financial education. J Consum Aff 39(1):195–214
Frazzini A (2006) The disposition effect and underreaction to news. J Financ 61(4):2017–2046
Freitas A, Higgins ET (2002) Enjoying goal-directed action: the role of regulatory fit. Psychol Sci 13(1):1–6
French K, Poterba J (1991) Investor diversification and international equity markets. Am Econ Rev 81(2):222–226
Frick RW (1995) Accepting the null hypothesis. Mem Cogn 23(1):132–138
Friedman RS, Förster J (2001) The effects of promotion and prevention cues on creativity. J Pers Soc Psychol 81(6):1001
Froot KA, Dabora EM (1999) How are stock prices affected by the location of trade? J Financ Econ 53(2):189–216
Ganster DC, Hennessey HW, Luthans F (1983) Social desirability response effects: Three alternative models. Acad Manage J 26(2):321–331
Gärling T, Kirchler E, Lewis A, Van Raaij F (2009) Psychology, financial decision making, and financial crises. Psychol Sci Public Interest 10(1):1–47
Garner A (1988) Has the stock market crash reduced consumer spending? Fed Reserve Bank Kansas City Econ Rev
Gibbons MR, Hess P (1981) Day of the week effects and asset returns. J Bus 54(4):579–596
Goetzmann WN, Kumar A (2001) Equity portfolio diversification, NBER working paper no. 8686. National Bureau of Economic Research
Goldberg HJ, Wichansky AM (2003) The mind's eye: cognitive and applied aspects of eye movement research. In: Hyönä J, Radach R, Deubel H (eds) Eye tracking in usability evaluation: a practitioner's guide. Elsevier, Amsterdam, pp 493–516
Grable JE (2000) Financial risk tolerance and additional factors that affect risk taking in everyday money matters. J Bus Psychol 14(4):625–630
Grant DA (1962) Testing the null hypothesis and the strategy and tactics of investigating theoretical models. Psychol Rev 69(1):54
Gray JA (1990) Brain systems that mediate both emotion and cognition. Cogn Emot 4(3):268–288
Gunnarsson J, Wahlund R (1997) Household financial strategies in Sweden: an exploratory study. J Econ Psychol 18(2–3):201–233
Harrison T (1994) Mapping customer segments for personal financial services. Int J Bank Mark 12(8):17–25
Haws KL, Dholakia U, Bearden WO (2010) An assessment of chronic regulatory focus measures. J Mark Res 47(5):967–982
Hens T, Vlcek M (2011) Does prospect theory explain the disposition effect? J Behav Financ 12(3):141–157

Herman A, Reiter-Palmon R (2011) The effect of regulatory focus on idea generation and idea evaluation. Psychol Aesthetics Creativity Arts 5(1):13
Higgins ET (1998) Promotion and prevention: regulatory focus as a motivational principle. In: Zanna MP (ed) Advances in experimental social psychology, vol 30. Academic Press, San Diego, pp 1–46
Higgins ET (2000) Making a good decision: value from fit. Am Psychol 55(11):1217–1230
Higgins ET (2002) How self-regulation creates distinct values: the case of promotion and prevention decision making. J Consum Psychol 12(3):177–191
Higgins ET (2005) Value from regulatory fit. Curr Dir Psychol Sci 14(4):209–213
Higgins ET, Bond RN, Klein RL, Strauman TJ (1986) Self-discrepancies and emotional vulnerability: how magnitude, accessibility, and type of discrepancy influence affect. J Pers Soc Psychol 51(1):5–15
Higgins ET, Roney CJR, Crowe E, Hymes C (1994) Ideal versus ought predilections for approach and avoidance: distinct self-regulatory systems. J Pers Soc Psychol 66(2):276–286
Higgins ET, Shah J, Friedman RS (1997) Emotional responses to goal attainment: Strength of regulatory focus as moderator. J Pers Soc Psychol 72(March):515–525
Hilgert MA, Hogarth JM, Beverly SG (2003) Household financial management: The connection between knowledge and behavior. Fed Reserve Bull 89
Hirshleifer D (2001) Investor psychology and asset pricing. J Financ 56:1533–1597
Hirshleifer D, Shumway T (2003) Good day sunshine: stock returns and the weather. J Financ 58(3):1009–1032
Hoffman JE (1998) Visual attention and eye movements. Attention 119–153
Holsanova J (2006) Dynamics of picture viewing and picture description. Adv Conscious Res 67:235
Hong H, Stein JC (1999) A unified theory of underreaction, momentum trading, and overreaction in asset markets. J Financ 54(6):2143–2184
Hong H, Kubik JD, Solomon A (2000) Security analysts' career concerns and herding of earnings forecasts. RAND J Econ 31(1):121–144
Hsee C, Weber E (1999) Cross-national differences in risk preference and lay predictions. J Behav Decis Making 12
Huberman G (2001) Familiarity breeds investment. Rev Financ Stud 14(3):659–680
Huston SJ (2010) Measuring financial literacy. J Consum Aff 44(2):296–316
Idson LC, Liberman N, Higgins ET (2011) Distinguishing gains from non losses and losses from non gains: a regulatory focus perspective on hedonic intensity. J Pers Soc Psychol 101(4): 720–736
Imbens G, Rubin D, Sacerdote B (2001) Estimating the effect of unearned income on labor earnings, savings, and consumption: Evidence from a survey of lottery players. Am Econ Rev 91(4):778–794
Janiszewski C (1998) The influence of display characteristics on visual exploratory search behavior. J Consum Res 25(3):290–301
Jegadeesh N, Titman S (1993) Returns to buying winners and selling losers: implications for stock market efficiency. J Financ 48(1):65–91
Jegadeesh N, Titman S (2001) Momentum. Ann Rev Financ Econ 3(1):493–509
Jegadeesh N, Titman S (2001) Profitability of momentum strategies: an evaluation of alternative explanations. J Financ 56(2):699–720
Jensen MC (1978) Some anomalous evidence regarding market efficiency. J Financ Econ 6(2/3):95–101
Jianakoplos NA, Bernasek A (1998) Are women more risk averse? Econ Inq 36(4):620–630
Jonas E, Schulz-Hardt S, Frey D (2005) Giving advice or making decisions in someone else's place: the influence of impression, defense, and accuracy motivation on the search for new information. Pers Soc Psychol Bull 31(7):977–990
Jones CS, Pomorski L (2002) Investing in disappearing anomalies. Working paper

Jung HS, Yoon HH (2015) Understanding regulatory focuses: the role of employees' regulatory focus in stress coping styles, and turnover intent to a five-star hotel. Int J Contemp Hospitality Manage 27(2):283–307

Just MA, Carpenter PA (1976) Eye fixations and cognitive processes. Cogn Psychol 8(4):441–480

Just MA, Carpenter PA (1980) A theory of reading: from eye fixations to comprehension. Psychol Rev 87(4):329–354

Kacmar KM, Tucker R (2014) The moderating effect of supervisor's behavioral integrity on the relationship between regulatory focus and impression management. J Bus Ethics 1–12

Kahneman D (2012) A proposal to deal with questions about priming effects. Nature. Retrieved 10 Oct 2013, from http://www.nature.com/polopoly_fs/7.6716.1349271308!/suppinfoFile/Kahneman%20Letter.pdf

Kahneman D, Tversky A (1979) Prospect theory: an analysis of decision under risk. Econometrica 47(2):263–291

Karn K, Goldberg J, McConkie G, Rojna W, Salvucci D, Senders J, Wooding D (2000) "Saccade pickers" versus "fixation pickers": the effect of eye tracking instrumentation on research. Paper presented at the Proceedings of the Eye Tracking Research and Applications Symposium 2000, New York

Ke D, Ng L, Wang Q (2009) Home bias in foreign investment decisions. J Int Bus Stud 41(6): 960–979

Keim DB (1983) Size-related anomalies and stock return seasonality: further empirical evidence. J Financ Econ 12(1):13–32

Keim DB, Stambaugh RF (1983) A further investigation of the weekend effect in stock returns. J Financ 39(3):819–835

Keller C, Siegrist M (2006) Money attitude typology and stock investment. J Behav Financ 7(2):88–96

Keller PA (2006) Regulatory focus and efficacy of health messages. J Consum Res 33(1):109–114

Khan U, Dhar R, Wertenbroch K (2005) A behavioral decision theoretic perspective on hedonic and utilitarian choice. In: Ratneshwar S, Mick DG (eds) Inside consumption: frontiers of research on consumer motives, goals, and desires. Routledge

Kim C-W, Park J (1994) Holiday effects and stock returns: further evidence. J Financ Quant Anal 29(1)

Kirmani A, Zhu RJ (2007) Vigilant against manipulation: the effect of regulatory focus on the use of persuasion knowledge. J Mark Res 44(4):688–701

Klenk MM, Strauman TJ, Higgins ET (2011) Regulatory focus and anxiety: a self-regulatory model of GAD-depression comorbidity. Pers Individ Differ 50(7):935–943

Knutson B, Bossaerts P (2007) Neural antecedents of financial decisions. J Neurosci 27(31): 8174–8177

Kray LJ (2000) Contingent weighting in self–other decision making. Organ Behav Hum Decis Process 83:82–106

Krivelyova A, Robotti C (2003) Playing the field: geomagnetic storms and the stock market. Fed Reserve Bank Atlanta Working Pap (5b)

Krueger TM, Kennedy WF (1990) An examination of the super bowl stock market predictor. J Financ 45(2):691–697

Kuhnen CM, Knutson B (2005) The neural basis of financial risk taking. Neuron 47(5):763–770

Lam TWH, Chiu CY (2002) The motivational function of regulatory focus in creativity. J Creative Behav 36(2):138–150

Langevoort DC (1996) Selling hope, selling risk: some lessons for law from behavioral economics about stockbrokers and sophisticated customers. Calif Law Rev 84(3):627–701

Latimer AE, Rivers SE, Rench TA, Katulak NA, Hicks A, Hodorowski JK, Salovey P (2008) A field experiment testing the utility of regulatory fit messages for promoting physical activity. J Exp Soc Psychol 44(3):826–832

Lee C, Shleifer A, Thaler RH (1991) Investor sentiment and the closed fund puzzle. J Financ 46(1):75–109

Lee AY, Aaker JL, Gardner WL (2000) The pleasures and pains of distinct self-construals: the role of interdependence in regulatory focus. J Pers Soc Psychol 78(6):1122–1134
Levy SJ (1981) Intepreting consumer mythology: a structural approach to consumer behavior. J Mark 45(6):49–61
Levy H, Levy M (2004) Prospect theory and mean-variance analysis. Rev Financ Stud 17(4):1015–1041
Liberman N, Idson LC, Camacho CJ, Higgins ET (1999) Promotion and prevention choices between stability and change. J Pers Soc Psychol 77(6):1135–1145
Lin H-F, Shen F (2012) Regulatory focus and attribute framing: Evidence of compatibility effects in advertising. Int J Advertising 31(1):169–188
List JA (2003) Does market experience eliminate market anomalies? Q J Econ 118(1):41–71
Lockwood P, Jordon CH, Kunda Z (2002) Motivation by positive or negative role models: regulatory focus determines who will best inspire us. J Pers Soc Psychol 83(4):854–864
Lohse GL (1997) Consumer eye movement patterns on yellow pages advertising. J Advertising 26(1):61–73
Loughran T, Ritter JR (2002) Why don't issuers get upset about leaving money on the table in IPOs? Rev Financ Stud 15(2):413–443
Lusardi A (2003) Saving and the effectiveness of financial education. Pension Res Counc Working Pap (14)
Lusardi A (2008) Financial literacy: an essential tool for informed consumer choice? NBER Working Paper No. 14084. National Bureau of Economic Research
Lusardi A, Mitchell OS, Curto V (2010) Financial literacy among the young. J Consum Aff 44(2):358–380
Maccoby EE, Maccoby N (1954) The interview: a tool of social science. In: Lindzey G (ed) handbook of social psychology, vol 1. Addison-Wesley, Cambridge, pp 449–487
Mandel N (2003) Shifting selves and decision making: the effects of self-construal priming on consumer risk-taking. J Consum Res 30(1):30–40
Mandell L (2008) Financial literacy of high school students. In: Handbook of consumer finance research. Springer, Berlin, pp 163–183
Markowitz HM (1952) Portfolio selection. J Financ 7(1):77–91
Markowitz HM (1959) Portfolio selection: efficient diversification of investments. Yale University Press, pp 317–336
Maslow AH, Frager R, Fadiman J (1970) Motivation and personality, vol 2. Harper & Row, New York
Matthey A (2010) The influence of priming on reference states. Games 1(1):34–52
Mehra R, Prescott EC (1985) The equity premium: a puzzle. J Monetary Econ 15(2):145–161
Mehta CR, Patel NR, Tsiatis AA (1984) Exact significance testing to establish treatment equivalence with ordered categorical data. Biometrics 40(3):819–825
Morris LA (2012) Communicating therapeutic risks. Springer Science & Business Media
Morse A, Shive S (2011) Patriotism in your portfolio. J Financ Markets 14(2):411–440
Naghi LE, Covrig M, Federovici A (2015). Impact of financial crisis on the decision making process for insurance consumers. Theor Appl Econ 22(1(602), Spring):301–310
Nederhof AJ (1985) Methods of coping with social desirability bias: a review. Eur J Soc Psychol 15(3):263–280
Nocera J (2009) Poking holes in a theory on markets. Retrieved 9 May, 2013, from http://www.nytimes.com/2009/06/06/business/06nocera.html?pagewanted=all
Noctor M, Stoney S, Stradling S (1992) Financial literacy: a discussion of concepts and competences of financial literacy and opportunities for its introduction into young people's learning. Nat Found Educ Res
Nordlund M (2009) The effects of priming on personality self-reports: challenges and opportunities

Nordlund M, Snell A (2006) Improving criterion-related validities with instructions to applicants: a good idea that actually worked. Presented at the annual meeting of the society for industrial and organizational psychology, Dallas, TX

Odean T (1999) Do investors trade too much? Am Econ Rev 89(5):1279–1298

Olsen RA, Cox CM (2001) The influence of gender on the perception and response to investment risk: the case of professional investors. J Psychol Financ Markets 2(1):29–36

Oppewal H (2011) Experimental research. In: Sirakaya-Turk E (ed) Research methods for leisure, recreation, and tourism. Wallingford, Oxfordshire England, CABI, Cambridge

Oyserman D, Lee SW (2008) Does culture influence what and how we think? Effects of priming individualism and collectivism. Psychol Bull 134(2):311

Park S-Y, Morton CR (2015) The role of regulatory focus, social distance, and involvement in anti-high-risk drinking advertising: a construal-level theory perspective. J Advertising 1–11

Pashler H, Coburn N, Harris CR (2012) Priming of social distance? Failure to replicate effects on social and food judgments. PloS one 7(8):e42510

Peltier BD, Walsh JA (1990) An investigation of response bias in the chapman scales. Educ Psychol Measur 50(4):803–815

Pentina I, Taylor DG (2013) Regulatory focus and daily-deal message framing: are we saving or gaining with groupon? J Interact Advertising 13(2):67–75

Pfattheicher S (2015) A regulatory focus perspective on reputational concerns: the impact of prevention-focused self-regulation. Motiv Emot

Pham T, Avnet T (2004) Ideals and oughts and the reliance on affect versus substance in persuasion. J Consum Res 30(4):503–518

Pham T, Chang HH (2010) Regulatory focus, regulatory fit, and the search and consideration of choice alternatives. J Consum Res 37(4):626–640

Podsakoff PM, MacKenzie SB, Lee J-Y, Podsakoff NP (2003) Common method biases in behavioral research: a critical review of the literature and recommended remedies. J Appl Psychol 88(5):879

Polivy J, Herman CP (2002) If at first you don't succeed: false hopes of self-change. Am Psychol 57(9):677–689

Polman E (2010) Information distortion in self–other decision making. J Exp Soc Psychol 46 (2):432–435

Polman E (2012) Effects of self-other decision making on regulatory focus and choice overload. J Pers Soc Psychol 102(5):980–993

Polman E, Emich KJ (2011) Decisions for others are more creative than decisions for the self. Pers Soc Psychol Bull 37(4):492–501

Pompian M (2012) Behavioral finance and investor types. Private Wealth Manage Feature Art 2012(1):1–3

Poole A, Ball LJ (2005) Eye tracking in human-computer interaction and usability research: current status and future prospects. In: Ghaoui C (ed) Encyclopedia of Human computer interaction. Idea Group Reference

Powell M, Ansic D (1997) Gender differences in risk behaviour in financial decision-making: an experimental analysis. J Econ Psychol 18(6):605–628

Rayner K, Pollatsek A, Ashby J, Clifton C Jr (2011) Psychology of reading, 2nd edn. Psychology Press

Riley W, Chow KV (1992) Asset allocation and individual risk aversion. Financ Anal J 48(6):32–37

Roese NJ, Hur T, Pennington GL (1999) Counterfactual thinking and regulatory focus implications for action versus inaction and sufficiency versus necessity. J Pers Soc Psychol 77(6):1109–1120

Roney CJR, Higgins ET, Shah J (1995) Goals and framing: how outcome focus influences motivation and emotion. Pers Soc Psychol Bull 21(11):1151–1160

Rooij MV, Lusardi A, Alessie R (2007) Financial literacy and stock market participation. NBER working paper no. 13565. National Bureau of Economic Research

Rooij MV, Lusardi A, Alessie R (2012) Financial literacy, retirement planning and household wealth. Econ J 122(560):449–478
Rosbergen E, Pieters R, Wedel M (1997) Visual attention to advertising: a segment-level analysis. J Consum Res 24(3):305–314
Rowley J (1996) Motivation and academic staff in higher education. Qual Assur Educ 4(3):11–16
Rowlingson K, McKay S (2005) Attitudes to inheritance in Britain. The Policy Press, Bristol
Rozeff MS, Kinney WR Jr (1976) Capital market seasonality: the case of stock returns. J Financ Econ 3:379–402
Saldaña J (2012) The coding manual for qualitative researchers. SAGE Publications Limited, London
Salvucci DD, Goldberg HJ (2000) Identifying fixations and saccades in eye-tracking protocols. Paper presented at the Proceedings of the Eye Tracking Research and Applications Symposium 2000, New York
Samuelson P (1965) Proof that properly anticipated prices fluctuate randomly. Ind Manage Rev 6(2):41–49
Scholer AA, Zou X, Fujita K, Stroessner SJ, Higgins ET (2010) When risk seeking becomes a motivational necessity. J Pers Soc Psychol 99(2):215–231
Sewell M (2010) Behavioural finance. Retrieved 19, Apr 2013, from http://www.behaviouralfinance.net/behavioural-finance.pdf
Shah J, Higgins ET (2001) Regulatory concerns and appraisal efficiency: the general impact of promotion and prevention. J Pers Soc Psychol 80(5):693–705
Shanks DR, Newell BR, Lee EH, Balakrishnan D, Ekelund L, Cenac Z, Moore C (2013) Priming intelligent behavior: an elusive phenomenon. PloS one 8(4):e56515
Shavit T, Giorgetta C, Shani Y, Ferlazzo F (2010) Using an eye tracker to examine behavioural biases in investment tasks: an experimental study. J Behav Financ 11(4):185–194
Shefrin H, Statman M (1984) Explaining investor preference for cash dividends. J Financ Econ 13(2):253–282
Shefrin H, Statman M (1985) The disposition to sell winners too early and ride losers too long: theory and evidence. J Financ 40(3):777–790
Sheth JN (1970) Are there differences in dissonance reduction behavior between students and housewives? J Mark Res 7(2):243–245
Shiller RJ (1981) Do stock prices move too much to be justified by subsequent changes in dividends? Am Econ Rev 71(3):421–436
Shiller RJ, Fischer S, Friedman BM (1984) Stock prices and social dynamics. Brookings Pap Econ Act 1984(2):457–510
Solnik B, Zuo L (2012) A global equilibrium asset pricing model with home preference. Manage Sci 58(2):273–292
Som A, Lee YH (2012) The joint effects of choice assortment and regulatory focus on choice behavior. Int J Res Mark 29(2):202–209
Statman M (2008) What is behavioral finance? In: Fabozzi FJ (ed) Handbook of Finance, vol II. Wiley, Hoboken
Sterne JA, Gavaghan D, Egger M (2000) Publication and related bias in meta-analysis: power of statistical tests and prevalence in the literature. J Clin Epidemiol 53(11):1119–1129
Stovall R (1989) The super bowl predictor. Financ World 158:72
Strandvall T (2013) Tobii eye tracker training (powerpoint slides)
Starr RG, Fernandez KV (2007) The Mindcam methodology: perceiving through the native's eye. Qual Market Res Int J 10(2):168–182
Sun Q, Tong WHS (2010) Risk and the January effect. J Bank Financ 34(5):965–974
Surveys of Consumers (2001) Retrieved 24 May 2013, from Thomson Reuters/University of Michigan http://thomsonreuters.com/products_services/financial/financial_products/a-z/umichigan_surveys_of_consumers/

Taleb NN (2010) The Black Swan: the impact of the highly improbable fragility. Random House Digital, Inc.

Tesar LL, Werner IM (1995) Home bias and high turnover. J lnt Money Financ 14(4):467–492

Thaler RH (1993) Introduction. In: Thaler RH (ed) Advances in behavioral finance. Russell Sage Foundation, New York, p 597

Thaler RH, Bondt WFMD (1995) Financial decision-making in markets and firms: A behavioral perspective. In: Jarrow R (ed) Handbooks in OR and MS, vol 9. Elsevier Science B.V.

Trueman B (1994) Analyst forecasts and herding behavior. Review of Financial Studies 7(1): 97–124

Tversky A, Kahneman D (1992) Advances in prospect theory: Cumulative representation of uncertainty. J Risk Uncertainty 5(4):297–323

Upton GJ (1992) Fisher's exact test. J Roy Stat Soc Ser A Stat Soc 395–402

Victoravich LM (2010) Overly optimistic? Investor sophistication and the role of affective reactions to financial information in investors' stock price judgements. J Behav Financ 11(1):1–10

Volcker P (2011) Financial reform: unfinished business. Retrieved 5th April, 2013, from http://www.nybooks.com/articles/archives/2011/nov/24/financial-reform-unfinished-business/

Wagland SP, Taylor S (2009) When it comes to financial literacy, is gender really an issue? Australas Account Bus Financ J 3(1):13

Wan W, Hong J, Sternthal B (2009) The effect of regulatory orientation and decision strategy on brand judgements. J Consum Res 35(6):1027–1039

Waneryd KE (2001) Stock market psychology: how people value and trade stocks. Edward Elgar, Cheltenham, United Kingdom

Wang J, Lee AY (2006) The role of regulatory focus in preference construction. J Mark Res 43(1):28–38

Watson J, McNaughton M (2007) Gender differences in risk aversion and expected retirement benefits. Financ Anal J 63(4):52–62

Weber E, Hsee C (1998) Cross-cultural differences in risk perception, but cross-cultural similarities in attitudes towards perceived risk. Manage Sci 44(9):1205–1217

Weber E, Hsee C (2000) Culture and individual judgment and decision making. Appl Psychol 49(1):32–61

Wermers R (1999) Mutual fund herding and impact on stock prices. J Financ 54(2):581–622

Willis L (2008) Against Financial Literacy Education. Iowa Law Rev 94:197

Wilson WR, Miller H (1964) A note on the inconclusiveness of accepting the null hypothesis. Psychol Rev 71(3):238

Winterheld HA, Simpson JA (2015) Regulatory focus and the interpersonal dynamics of romantic partners' personal goal discussions. J Pers

Wolfradt U, Pretz JE (2001) Individual differences in creativity: personality, story writing, and hobbies. Eur J Pers 15(4):297–310

Wood R, Zaichkowsky JL (2004) Attitudes and trading behavior of stock market investors: A segmentation approach. J Behav Financ 5(3):170–179

Wright RD, Ward LM (2008) Orienting of attention. Oxford University Press

Yarbus AL, Riggs LA (1967) Eye movements and vision, vol 2. Plenum press New York

Yates D, Moore D, Starnes DS (2002) The practice of statistics: TI-83/89 graphing calculator enhanced. Macmillan

Yong E (2012) Replication studies: bad copy. Nature 485(7398):298

Yuan K, Zheng L, Zhu Q (2006) Are investors moonstruck? Lunar phases and stock returns. J Empirical Financ 13(1):1–23

Zagorsky JL (2013) Do people save or spend their inheritances? Understanding what happens to inherited wealth. J Fam Econ Issues 34(1):64–76

Zhang S, Higgins ET, Chen G (2011) Managing others like you were managed: How prevention focus motivates copying interpersonal norms. J Pers Soc Psychol 100(4):647

Zhao G, Pechmann C (2007) The impact of regulatory focus on adolescents' response to antismoking advertising campaigns. J Mark Res 44(4):671–687
Zhou R, Pham T (2004) Promotion and prevention across mental accounts: when financial products dictate consumers' investment goals. J Consum Res 31(1):125–135
Zhu RJ, Meyers-Levy J (2007) Exploring the cognitive mechanism that underlies regulatory focus effects. J Consum Res 34(1):89–96

MIX
Papier aus verantwortungsvollen Quellen
Paper from responsible sources
FSC® C105338

If you have any concerns about our products,
you can contact us on
ProductSafety@springernature.com

In case Publisher is established outside the EU,
the EU authorized representative is:
Springer Nature Customer Service Center GmbH
Europaplatz 3, 69115 Heidelberg, Germany

Printed by Libri Plureos GmbH
in Hamburg, Germany